LANDMARK first published 1982 by Theatre Action Press
c/o Department of Literature, University of Essex
Wivenhoe Park, Colchester CO4 3SQ

Copyright © Steve Gooch 1982
Songs: lyrics copyright © Steve Gooch 1982
     music copyright © Nicolle Freni 1982
Introduction copyright © Theatre Action Press 1982

All rights whatsoever in this play are strictly reserved and applications to perform it, etc., must be made, in advance, before rehearsals begin, to Margaret Ramsay Ltd., 14a Goodwin Court, St. Martins Lane, London WC2.
Rights to perform the music printed in this edition of *Landmark* may be obtained from Nicolle Freni c/o Theatre Action Press.

Theatre Action Press acknowledges the financial assistance of the Eastern Arts Association in the publishing of *Landmark*.

ISBN 90057511 5

Printed by the University of Essex

LANDMARK

a play by Steve Gooch

ESSEX UNIVERSITY NEW PLAYS
Editor: Leslie Bell
THEATRE ACTION PRESS

LANDMARK was first performed as an M.A. Drama group Directed Project by the Theatre Underground at Essex University Theatre, Colchester on 1st December 1980, directed by Charlie Langdon-Mead.

Carol	Ruth Shade
Sandy	Liz Kettle
Gary	Paul Brightwell
Jim	Miles Ridley
Di	Wanda Zyborska
Don	Ian Barnes
George	Leslie Bell
Ted	Hugh Lambert
Joyce Knight	Sara Green
Les	Ed O'Regan
T.V. Director	Charles Butler
T.V. Technician	Charlie Langdon-Mead
Design	Helen Napper, Sue Osman
Songs:	Lyrics — Steve Gooch
	Music — Nicolle Freni
Administration	Richard Upton
Production Manager	Martin Pudney
Lighting	Bert Bearcroft, William Burdett-Coutts, Dave Edwards, Andy Obeid
Sound	Rachel Culley, Penny McHale
Set Construction	Stuart Mead
Stage Managers	Pauline Jones, Dot Murphy, Sue Krantz
Wardrobe	Nicola Sugden, Anne Reynolds, Diana Antony

Introduction

Based on documentation by the 1980-81 M.A. drama group

ON THE PLAY

It is no doubt deliberate that the play's title should have many different resonances: it refers to the barn in which *Landmark* is set, to the effect of technology on the soil; to a term likely to be employed in strategic bombing operations and — this is the play's unifying factor — to each occasion in people's lives when external events overtake them, or when they compromise their principles, or when they finally have the courage and will to protest for a right to a say in determining their own destinies. In the first draft the TV Director stated in Scene Six: "If anything happened, we'd have a scoop ... . We're supposed to be neutral ... ." In the finished version, this read: "If anything happened we'd scoop the other side ... . We're supposed to be neutral ... ." With the extra degree of self-interest in this version, one senses the author's grave doubts about the outcome of the arms race.

The technological advancement of the human race without the development of a corresponding moral sense has brought the species to the brink of self-destruction. This issue raises deeper and darker questions about the instinctive and tribal forces at play within the species. Hence, the tribal and ritualistic elements in the gang's play. Hence, the importance of the Oath ("Never to grow up like our parents") against which all the members of the gang's subsequent actions are judged. Hence the instinctive rather than rational basis of Sandy and Carol's decisions to protest. Hence the ambiguous attitude towards technology in the shape of the TV crew. Hence the typing of the 'outsiders' — Joyce, Les and Ted. They are members of a different gang or tribe, and are therefore to be regarded with suspicion. This hypothesis also goes some way towards explaining Carol's irrational outbursts of anger, the 'group fantasy' aspect of the flashback sequences, and the role of George as Custodian of the oath. This instinctive, tribal aspect of man's nature is viewed ambiguously: it can be positive when it fosters a sense of community (Carol's decision to help George) or destructive when it leads to the installation of a cruise missile base. (1)

Landmark does not have a dramatic climax or a resolution. Climax is often approached, as in the arguments between Jim and Don, Don and Carol, and in Scene Five between Gary and Don; but conflict is never resolved in the traditional way because it is not allowed to become an individualistic battle of two wills. There is always the group will, which intervenes, and it is the dissenter to this will who must either leave the group or change. The action continues through the group, the dissenter becomes peripheral. Change is shown more or less in the individual characters but is at its most radical and constant in the group as a whole. From some old friends meeting for a reunion, (they are not initially united), they move through a growing political awareness and sense of responsibility to become a (smaller) group of committed activists. The whole structure of the play is based on social rather than individual interaction. Almost all the action on stage takes place between four or more people. These people are seen in terms of their social status, they are defined by their function in society. This is more true in the second half of the play than the first. The first half deals with individual character development, particularly in the flashback scenes and in the personal revelations in Scene One. By showing how personal issues can become political, as when Carol's sympathy for George makes her decide to join the campaign, the personal is shown to be political. This basic premise of feminism is an underlying theme throughout this play, and indeed Steve Gooch's work in general. The female characters in *Landmark*, except for Joyce Knight, show a growing awareness of their position, and a positive aptitude for change. They play major roles throughout the campaign, and if not always the most vocal members, they tend to be the most consistent — as Carol says: "I hope the blokes realise who the backbone of this operation is."

It is significant that in the final scene it is the three women who are carrying on with the radical spearhead of the campaign, along with Gary, the least aggressively 'male' of the three men. In a way Jim and Don are examples in society of the same type of individualistic aggressive man. The changes which take place in Jim, Carol and Sandy show that although the characters are defined by their positions in society, they are not totally controlled by them. As a socialist Steve Gooch uses Realism because it is a form which admits this possibility for change. The characters can change not only themselves, but also each other and therefore society. (2)

Gooch's drama characteristically deals with a group of individuals who are representative of the society that formed them, and whose inter-play exposes issues of relevance to the audience that views it. It is this social aspect of Gooch's drama, with its implicit faith in Man as a social animal, capable of moral evolution, that forms the core of the author's Realism. And yet the influence of the Epic Theatre is evident in the 'pointing' of entrances and exits in *Landmark*. Characters are observed to be approaching from a distance before they actually enter; their mood and appearance is described; there is speculation on what news they bring, and how it is likely to affect the internal dynamic of the group on stage. When they exit, their attitudes, opinions and the consequences of their proposed courses of action are analysed. In opting for a wholly 'realistic' approach to the design of the set, the Theatre Underground's production of *Landmark* failed to capitalise upon the possibilities of this aspect of the script. The approach and departure of characters was visible, it is true, but not for a sufficiently prolonged period. Yet, in the early stages of rehearsal, the actors playing Joyce, Les and Ted found themselves instinctively making just such prolonged entrances before the inevitable rehearsal process of waiting and repetition erased such movements. The seal was set upon the brief entrance and the rapid departure when the physical construction of the set eliminated such a possibility. (1)

Language and Characterisation in Landmark

The primary Realistic element in Gooch's work is his use of language. His plays are not "literary" pieces; they are stage-plays based on regional working-class dialect.

Gooch studied languages for some years, and throughout the process of rehearsal and rewrites on *Landmark*, his training became apparent in his meticulous attention to fine detail: "I say!" became "Stone me!"; "Anyway" became "But" or "Really". Gooch's characteristic dramatic language consists of cleverly orchestrated interchanges of apparent simplicity and, usually, brief duration. Their effect is gradual and cumulative: unobtrusively, they reveal individual character and motivation, and broader alliances and disputes within the social group he is treating. There are no soliloquies in the manner of Renaissance or Romantic art because of Gooch's insistence on the essentially *social* purpose, function and identity of man.

This approach to dramatic language means that it is only when *action* is introduced, when his characters take the stage as flesh and blood, that the play comes to life. The best scenes in *Landmark* are those rich in movement and confrontation (like, say, the 'flashback' scenes) where the language rises to meet the requirements of the action.(1)

The script consists almost entirely of apparently simple 'one-liners' which contrast not only with the form of most conventional bourgeois theatre, but also with agit-prop exhortations and the conscious speeches of the epic theatre. This is a subtle device for delivering information and showing insight into character through social interaction while giving respect and attention to the way people actually talk — realizing the function of apparently superfluous "anyway"s, "well"s, "sort of"s and "you know"s. The sub-text thus formed is all-important in *Landmark*. Motivation is often suggested rather than made explicit, underlying attitudes are shown by casual allusions. For example Gary's attitude to mechanization is contained in his simple answer to Jim's baiting:
    Jim: Suppose you think the wheel was a big mistake an' all.
    Gary: Depends what it's on, Jim. (2)

Landmark allows audiences to study the words and actions of the characters simultaneously from two different points of view. As in life, so in *Landmark*, any action is like a small part in a large machine; it is moved by another part and itself sets in motion a third part (and sometimes others as well). In a play in which all attention is centred on one central character, undue emphasis (Gooch would say) is placed on that character as the chief cause of the events in the play, and the effects of those events on other characters are not examined in any detail. Furthermore, no account is taken of the consequences of actions performed in a social context for their originator; the ways in which they provoke reciprocal actions from other sources, the effects of which feed back into their lives and affect their subsequent behaviour. This two-way exchange between individuals and their social context is too often ignored in drama. In *Landmark* one sees a fascinating intermeshing of cause and effect; each character simultaneously influences and is influenced by the action of the play. In life, character and behaviour are flexible and vary according to the context in which they are manifested. We all behave differently in the presence of different people and therefore cannot be said to have one distinct, unvarying personality. To say that each person has such a personality is to ignore these differences in behaviour. Individuals in *Landmark* are characterised largely by reference to external aspects of their lives; their jobs or professions, their declared attitudes to the issues raised in the play, the character of their speech and so on.

All these points have a direct bearing on the use of language in the play, which is on the whole straightforward and fairly unsophisticated. There is no intellectual wordplay, no 'cleverness'. Not that *Landmark* is entirely free of rhetoric. Don, for example, has evolved a kind of rhetorical speech, having its origin in his natural forthrightness and the necessity of 'asking the difficult question', which is used powerfully (frequently compounded with sarcasm) to put over a point. But it never develops to such an extent that the audience is allowed to forget the context in which it is being used. Don's speeches are always terse rather than expansive and never become displays of declamatory virtuosity. An example chosen at random is his calculatedly unanswerable question in Scene Five: "Would you trust the Pentagon? ITT? Krupp?" In its context this is an extremely pointed and significant question, but it is only within that context that it can be understood.

Despite the absence of any overtly intellectualised use of language by the characters it must not be imagined that the play has little or no intellectual content. There is a continuous dialectic, a search for political, economic and ethical truth which is pursued through the 'action' of the play. The opinions of each character are articulated and tested but no hard and fast conclusions are reached as to their validity. Thus language is used not as a means of convincing audiences of truths of which the playwright is already convinced himself, but to articulate points of view which may then be tested by playwright and public alike. In the talk given during the performance week Steve Gooch stated that it was his intention in writing *Landmark* to use language 'physically'. During the improvisation period exercises were performed in which members of the group were required to convey meanings by purely physical means; these included charades and role-playing exercises. When, later on in the improvisations, non-verbal and verbal communication were combined in the same exercise, the group found that the two forms of communication could be used simultaneously with improved co-ordination — it became more natural and instinctive to combine words and actions — and that speech could not be regarded as more important than movement; in this sense speech was being used physically, i.e. to articulate states of being rather than to convey an elaborate verbal meaning.

However, the physical use of language to which Gooch referred has another explanation. The play deals with those factors which affect its characters' lives in direct and immediate ways; more specifically, economic and political factors. Language is seen as one of those factors that is a determinant of social behaviour in particular and of human actions generally. It is both an indicator of class and political outlook and is itself to some extent determined by them. The language people use affects their destinies just as physical factors do. Thus Joyce Knight's 'diplomatic' use of language (which serves to create a public image of practical concern but at the same time facilitates the evasion of awkward questions and the concealment of that which she does not want others to know) is seen to affect both her own life and those of the other characters in several ways. Firstly, as a tool of the politician's trade which has enabled her to reach her current position, i.e. as a determinant of her role in life; secondly, as an indicator of that role; thirdly, as a determinant of external events and the destinies of other people. The relatively sophisticated way in which she uses language for her own ends is demonstrated by the following passage which is her reply when asked what the land on which the barn stands is being bought for:—

"Well of course it's terribly difficult to get a straight answer on these things, but it does appear the Ministry is involved in several purchases connected with the rethink on Defence."(3)

What the language achieves is a unity, a classlessness and a naturalistic style which demands a reciprocal approach in the acting style. It is a useful adjunct to the writer's approach to characterisation; for in *Landmark*, although some characters attempt to show individuality they are ham-strung by the structure of the group, society, multi-nationals, the union, the Ministry of Defence, etc. They need the support of each other. The group, then, is more important than the individual in *Landmark* and it is important to consider the writer's work method in relation to this for characters are not worked on in isolation but in terms of their influence on one another. For this reason, Gooch doesn't prepare character sketches beforehand but lets the characters develop during the play in terms of the scope of the story: when the circumstances are contradictory, so too are the characters involved in them. This is well illustrated by the behaviour of Carol in Scene Two. She explodes upon the situation by attacking the group for going ahead with preparations for the rally and concludes the outburst by hurling Gary's thoughtfully prepared game to the floor. Only five minutes later she is closing the scene with "Food and drink I can organise from the pub, we can make it our headquarters". What has changed Carol is George's passive acceptance of his potential homelessness through eviction. The situation has changed and Carol has changed with it.

It was this changeability in Carol which provided me with my greatest problems when preparing the part. She is perpetually contradictory: it is she who organises the reunion, the catalyst therefore for the narrative of the whole play yet she is constantly and forcefully reprimanding Don, Gary and Di for harassing Jim. She complains about her husband Eddie, the hard work involved in running the pub and she is regretful about giving up her singing yet when Sandy suggests that Carol joins her in a spree she says "Can't leave the pub, can I". In Scene Three she admits that she and Sandy tended to leave Di out of their friendship, yet minutes later she attacks Di for being "Don's bloody echo". In Scene Four she spends the first half getting things "off to a good start" by paying particular attention to Joyce Knight's (the M.P's) welfare and concludes the scene by rounding on Di, Don and Jim (her great friend in Scene One) and finally bursting into tears.

However it must be remembered that Carol is a do-er, a practical woman. She is used to having people tell their life stories over "four lagers". She knows how to organise the barn into something visually impressive for the rally, she knows how to get hold of the local M.P., and she knows that large, seemingly impersonal issues affect individuals — the nuclear arms race is a "moral issue". In Scene Five Carol is out of her depth, because a 'formal' debate is not something she is used to handling. The writer has described the important qualities in Carol as being her toughness, her warmheartedness, her adherence to traditional values and her openness to change.(4)

It is noticeable how, whilst characters disagree strongly with each other, they rarely misunderstand one another. They are on the whole quick on the uptake, and the principal idiom of the play is one of quick response. (5)

The Songs

The songs in *Landmark* are neither 'character songs', about a particular character's plight and often sung by her/him, nor are they songs that advance the plot. Their scope is much wider than the context of the play, although specific issues in the play are dealt with in them. In a meeting with the writer, Gooch expressed the need for the songs to be sung collectively — he was not in favour of a single voice — but he did feel that a song may 'point' to one or more characters. In his talk two months later on 'Theatre, the Collective Art' he stated: "Work on one character must always relate to interaction with other characters, plus the invisible outside of the play". In reference to the characterisation in *Landmark* specifically he stated, "We're looking at motive and effect, how the collective dynamic works". It is this 'collective' approach, always to view a character in the much broader setting of her/his class, social milieu, the society around her/him and its economic/political/ethical status that gives the songs their particular flavour. They are not sentimental about individuals, but they are not unemotional. The positive emotion stems from feelings of solidarity, most overtly in 'We're making it known', 'Reunion', and 'People who know how to care'. The power of emotion in the play does not come from romantic love relationships, deliberately missing. If a song points to one or more characters, it does so unobtrusively and by inference, and invariably in relation to the dynamic, larger issues that define her/his situation.

The songs also point to themes, such as 'use of the land', a major theme in *Landmark*, powerfully portrayed in 'We eat what we make', reinforced in the simpler 'It's there', and seen from a totally different angle in 'We're making it known', about activism in relation to the land. Another resonant theme, 'growing up', was in the unofficial theme song of *Landmark*, 'Growing', which appears at the beginning and end of the play. 'Growing' anticipates what we are to see in the play, providing such detail as the specific age of the adults looking back over their shoulders: "And by the time we're thirty/Our hopes all hang in rags." The songs may anticipate events, or reflect on them, or bridge the gap of past and present as with 'Getting older'.

A strong undercurrent of the play is the loss of solidarity, once based on common class and values in childhood, and the fragmentation caused by their generation's separation from the land and absorption into the conformist knot their parents were caught up in. That this knot is tied by capitalist bosses — those who clearly "do not know how to share" — is the inference.

In a music rehearsal, Gooch explained that a certain 'obliqueness' about the songs was deliberately there. They were meant to convey irony, not merely to reflect what actually happens. Often the opposite happens, as in 'Reunion', where the chorus makes two 'false' statements in the light of the play: the characters are not "all one again", nor does the Union necessarily "speak for all working men". This irony gives the songs a level of detachment from the action in the play that is useful. (6)

The Flashbacks

The group's aspirations are never made fully clear in the flashbacks. One can recognise certain areas of interest — Gary's desire to see George's new beet harvester, Don's regurgitation of his father's views on the value of unions, Jim's feeling that the others' attitude towards the gang is childish — but this is about as far as it goes. What *is* consistent is the power structure and character traits of the group — Don and Carol are as dominant as adults as they were as children, Di is still very much the "third" of the group of women, Don and Jim still bicker, Carol and Sandy are still close friends, Gary still has very little money. (4)

What we appear to have in these scenes, then, is a spontaneous group fantasy informing the audience about the history of the gang, its special relationship with

George, and the tribal and ritualistic aspects of its activities: the mingling of blood, cutting of hair and swearing of the oath. It is significant that *Landmark*'s director introduced a deliberately formal, unrealistic stage grouping at the mingling of blood. I, personally, was unsure of the decision to have real props (apples, stove, tin, coins, gang-book, chewing gum, packet of Durex, and so on) for these essentially unrealistic scenes. (1)

Gooch was concerned realistically to recreate the speech of young people. The first 'flashback' in Scene One demonstrates this particularly well. There is a continuous group dialogue between the members of the Red Mouth Gang in which they are all constantly competing with each other in order to make their voices heard. Their childish world is a microcosm of the political arena into which they set foot some years later when they start their campaign; there also they are fighting to be heard. Occasionally an exchange takes place between two individuals but it is normally very brief as the other characters are standing by eager to assert themselves again. (3)

IN PRODUCTION
The Workshops

Charlie Langdon-Mead approached the sessions with four basic preoccupations to do with the group of six old friends, although the other characters, in many ways 'outsiders' to the shared experience and intimacy of the 'gang', were occasionally dealt with.

(1) The interrelationships of a (given) group of people as it was in the past.
(2) The interrelationships of a (given) group of people as it is remembered in the present, with all the distortions of memory.
(3) The interrelationships of a (given) group of people as it is in the present, with the past in mind.
(4) The interrelationships of a (given) group of people as it develops in the present, independent of the past, with the future in mind.

The aim was to develop the relationships between the characters, rather than the characters themselves, in opposition to the individualistic approach of most bourgeois theatre.

Almost every workshop began with physical exercises, as did the actual rehearsals: exercises to develop balance, awareness of the individual's sense of space, extension exercises as a group to develop concentration and co-ordination, and trust exercises with blindfolds, those blindfolded letting themselves be led about and having to discern, for instance, a leader from a disrupter by touch alone.

The next step was a series of variations on 'Charades', which involved role-playing and expression, working towards non-verbal communication and an understanding of the significance of physicality on stage. We began by doing impressions of physical objects and moved on to abstract concepts. We played Charades in pairs and groups of three, adding expressive sounds that weren't words. Finally we used language while attempting to keep the emphasis on movement.

The theme of ritual object, (the knife, coins, hair, gang book and the piece of paper on which the oath is written) was suggested by improvisations based on significant objects remembered from our subjective adolescences. These ranged from a crucifix, a balaclava and a biro to Rolling Stones records and a Napoleonic bomb shelter. The improvisations led into the beginnings of character manipulation and we produced a series of interviews where the interviewee maintained a passive role enforced on them by only being able to answer 'yes' and 'no' consecutively. Individually, and then in groups, other members created characters in the second person for the first person. This developed into the setting up of trial situations where the person on trial was not informed as to the nature of the 'crime'. A similar method was used to give the characters a youthful past which was combined with the previous adult. After all these experiments in character building, the characters were put in the 'hot seat' and questioned to discover their understanding of the character they had been given. These characters were extended by the setting-up of meetings between them as old friends who have not seen each other for years. Other situations relevant to *Landmark* were also improvised.

After three weeks, the actual characters of *Landmark* were introduced. We had three sessions during the week in which we were divided into groups of twos and threes, more or less in our own final roles — the casting was decided by now, except for the roles of Jim and Don. The sessions consisted of improvisations in character on given subjects:—

Session 1
Group A. Carol and Sandy talking about men.
Group B. Don, Ted and Joyce on Labour Party politics.
Group C. Gary, George and Les on housing.
Group D. Di and Jim on the legal aspects of land.

Session 2
Group A. Carol and Don on people and politics.
Group B. Sandy and Gary on sex and politics.
Group C. Jim, Les and Ted on the relationship of big business to local councils.
Group D. Di, George and Joyce on land and politics.

Session 3
Group A. Jim, Don and Gary on men.
Group B. Carol, Di and Sandy on women.
Group C. Joyce, Ted and Les on government and NATO.
George was free-floating in Session 3 and passed from group to group intervening and linking them.

By the end of the week the final casting had been decided.

The final week of improvisations started with a rediscussion of the chronology of the play and an exploration of the gang as children and their responses to their parents. The main considerations for the week were:—

(1) Interrelationships of characters.
(2) Their environment and feelings of personal territory.
(3) Acting style, which was to reflect the cross of theatricality and realism within the play. The audience was not to be overtly recognized or called on.

From this final week it emerged that the flashback sequences, played by the same actors without costume changes, must be the group as they *remember* themselves — the group "play at" or improvise a memory of themselves at 14. The movement into flashback was to follow a sequence of (a) actual remembrance as a 30-year-old (b) leading into a remembrance as a 14-year-old to (c) possibly becoming that 14-year-old.

At the end of this final week of improvisations each character was again put in the hot seat and attempted to answer questions in character, with the background provided by the whole workshop period. (2)

REHEARSALS
The Characterisation of Carol: some questions of acting style

The acting style of the play was difficult to achieve. Since the play requires delicate ensemble playing it was vital that the cast were in keeping with one another stylistically. Lack of technique led to some disastrous under- and over-playing. Carol's switches from conciliation to emotional turbulence were difficult to make credible. She is the most overtly emotional character in the play and because of this it was perhaps a more difficult part to play than the others because the major problem was in rising to those emotional peaks without disturbing the flatter, more matter-of-fact approach which the other cast members could use.

In the first scene, for example, Carol displays excitement and nostalgia, a reverence for what the Barn means, yet within minutes she says "You two been setting the world to rights" and "Now come on you two" — lines which are a reprimand but which needed to be said without disturbing the nature of the reunion. I had also to switch from reflectiveness "So I went crawling back to Eddie. No more singing though" to active interest in the others "What I want to know is what everyone's been doin' with 'emselves".

The way I attempted to solve these problems was by making her emotionally consistent in the sense that I tried to show a Carol who was full of life, i.e. her laughter, her enthusiasm, her energy could give rise to her tears, her anger, her disappointment. I tried to make her confident in both her conciliation and her admonishment; a Carol who was not frightened of her volatility. I tried also to make her cheerful rather than comical and I did this by making her smile, particularly sympathetically. But it was the attitude of the other actors which allowed me to do this. As a company we were, I felt, united and generous towards one another. There were few tantrums. When I had a particularly difficult scene the others supported me by giving me their concentration and by feeding the essential cues and emotional responses in a sensitive and considered way. I hope that I succeeded in doing the same for them.

It was never a group decision to go for a realistic approach but, rather, the director's, and it seems to me that a more open approach to alternative acting styles would have liberated the actors in *Landmark*. A naturalistic approach was by no means the only one possible. It would have been interesting to experiment with caricature, for example, or to attempt a more stylised approach simply to see what effect that might have had on the sense of the play.

It was always difficult to make sense of a complex narrative, and an exercise used on Scene Five would have been useful if used elsewhere. It was the writer's idea to sit around in a circle and pin-point the 'beats' or most significant lines in the scene

The scene was then divided up into sections:—

1.	TED : "You don't mind?" to DON : "Maybe it's time we started"	Setting of the scene — allowing the audience to observe the atmosphere and nature of the new scene.
2.	GARY : "Oh?" to JIM : "We've got to be organised"	Discussion about the purpose of the evening — issues to be discussed.
3.	GARY : "Who by? You?" to DI'S ENTRANCE	Re-introduction of the tension between Jim, Gary and Di.

What this experiment did was to emphasise the key lines in the scene and to give the actors an understanding of the shifts in focus. A similar approach to the rest of the play would have enabled the actors to have a less tenuous hold of the narrative and would in turn have made for better focussing on the important moments in the play which would in turn have made the narrative clearer for the audience. It would also have assisted in pin-pointing climaxes, moments of tension, shifts in mood, all of which are vital in terms of an actor's understanding of the pacing of a role. An effect of this also would have been to make textual memory easier and faster.

There were occasions when I felt that I was being forced into playing the director's (more so than the writer's who had an open mind towards the *method* of characterisation) version of Carol's anger, Carol's distaste. Curiously it was my reaction to this firm direction which brought about a more satisfying form of acting. It so happened that I became alienated from Carol: I didn't "become" her — I was an actress presenting or imitating Carol. There was a strong degree of objectivity in my playing of her. I was aware of her faults as well as her strengths, aware of her context within the group and her function within the play. It was this realisation that was the most rewarding aspect of the whole project for me. I discovered, I think, a little of what Brecht wanted from his actors. Of course it is quite probable no-one noticed that in my playing but I did and it meant something to me. (4)

Offstage discussion

There were mixed viewpoints about the issues raised. We were not all ardent C.N.D., feminist, friends of the earth. But although there were varying degrees of commitment to these causes, no one involved in the production was actually against them, and there was a healthy running discussion carried on backstage and in the bar and restaurant. (2)

The Writer's Involvement

Gooch was sometimes present in an observatory capacity and, during the actual rehearsal period, would often constructively feed back immediate impressions to the cast or make written observations to the director on development of roles.

Initially it had been agreed that the company's involvement in rewriting processes was to be encouraged but that ultimate decisions and rewrites *must* be Gooch's prerogative. At certain stages of the rehearsal process his personal influence on the work in hand was apparent, generally in rapport with the director-company relationship.

At a recording session I observed, in the penultimate week of rehearsals, Gooch asserted major control of the handling of musical material, the director handling the technical side. (7)

The *Landmark* project benefited greatly from having the writer there. Unlike so many productions it was not a homage to a dead playwright, nor was it a production which was graced by a flying visit from a great guru. The writer was there a great deal of the time and never set himself up to be the only authority on his play or the guardian of the holy *Landmark*. (4)

On no occasion did I feel railroaded into playing music I disliked for a song, which I think was due to an artistic integrity in Gooch. His experience in collaboration and collective working were in evidence, because he was able to explain what he felt were the needs of the songs, receive my ideas about them, and laboriously plod on with me until we had both reached the same place. I felt no resentment at his disapproval of an idea, but rather the opposite — that it was an advantage to have the playwright there to assist in interpretation, and I think a profound respect grew between us because of our attitude toward the work and each other's domain within it. (6)

OPEN REHEARSALS

During the last week of rehearsals the public was invited to come in and watch, free, the process of theatre being produced. Not only to watch, but to comment, criticise, and ask questions of the cast, director, and playwright. The majority who accepted this invitation were drama students from schools and colleges in Essex, not merely from the immediate vicinity of Colchester. Although by this stage it was almost a finished product they were seeing, their comments materially altered some aspects of the production. Many came back the following week to see the play performed.

By 25th November we had a set and were ready to start open rehearsals in the theatre. Also during this week we obtained the considerable number of props required in the production and a lot of meticulous work done during these rehearsals was to do with integrating the props and also reblocking to accommodate the set and the different dimensions of the acting area from that of the rehearsal rooms. That is not to say that acting notes were not given. Actors had to re-adjust the volume of their voices to the larger space of the theatre in many scenes which had been rehearsed in an understated, low-key fashion. (5)

The purposes of the open rehearsals could be seen as: a means of bridging the gap between the intimacy of rehearsals and the theatrical consciousness needed for performance; a method of considering weaknesses or a lack of clarity in the characterisation, style of performance and ideas behind the play; an opportunity for the whole production group to reflect on the process of bringing a play from the bare text to performance. (4)

The majority of rehearsals in the final week were open. How useful or otherwise they were is debatable. Open rehearsals must expose the show and company to public view and comment prior to actual performance. Inevitably, though, by this stage much had been irrevocably consolidated and major changes —were they indeed possible — could be disastrous to company morale and the state of the show. Usually this is the period of final polish to the work firmly established throughout the whole rehearsal period rather than a period of flux where ideas arising from critical comment and discussion may be assimilated to any effect. In other words, the public are previewing a near-finished product. (7)

The kids were concerned with what we would look like with our costumes on, with what the props would look like. They tended to pick-up on the broader aspects of characterisation and be more interested in the development of the narrative. The adults, on the other hand, tended to be more concerned with the issues in the play. (4)

I was surprised that even the younger members of our audiences did not appear to be bored by the repetitious nature and minutiae of the proceedings, but were stimulated and prepared to articulate their criticisms. One or two of the children said they thought the attention to detail the most interesting insight into the rehearsal procedure — they had previously accepted the illusions of Realism without questioning its devices.

Just as the audience found the open rehearsals stimulating, so we in the cast found many of the points raised valuable, not to mention the positive tension generated by the presence of an audience, which minimized the danger of the cast's going stale after such a long period of rehearsal. The audience also expressed views on the accents used in the play, but because these views were contradictory they were not acted upon. One section of the audience maintained that the cast's accents were "posh", while another felt that our accents were "anti-educational"! At any rate it was too late in the rehearsal period for any extensive work to be done on accent, so any inconsistencies had to remain. (2)

Asked by one of the audience whether *Landmark* was a play of characters or of political ideas, Steve Gooch replied "It is both: it has a sort of message but it is not just a bottle with a ship in it." (5)

PROPS, SET, LIGHTING
Landmark is dominated by objects: cans of beer, crisps, apples, the contents of the gang's tin, Gary's spot-the-farmworker game, tables, bunting, jumble, posters for an exhibition, gin and tonics, a plate of cocktail savouries. It is vital that scenes are timed with the props to hand. (4)

The set's solid timbers were enhanced by the textured mellowings of the paintwork and the shading of the stage floor to define areas. The background combined reversed flats in the rear wall elevation with the clap-board effect of the side walls. The broken window in silhouette was an effective feature. Colourings harmonised paintwork and natural commodities, like the woodwork and straw bales, into an atmospheric rural whole offset by the ropes, tackle and machinery; the bright fertilizer bags and, later, the colourful bunting, giving visual relief.

The pre-production lighting relied on a bright cyclorama and could perhaps have gently pinpointed architectural features of the interior. The general interior lighting was warm and the hard white of the flash-back effects was in strong contrast. (7)

PERFORMANCE

The company had worked flat out in rehearsals and a warm-up till shortly before the time of the audience's arrival. Perhaps overstrain and maybe a sense of anti-climax flattened the opening night. In fact things went smoothly, if rather automatically, and whilst the director seemed disappointed, the writer was gratified sufficiently to comment that the production-dynamic had been mislaid during the evening but added his conviction that it would return as the run recharged energies and restored confidence in what had been positively achieved in the rehearsals.

The premiere of *Landmark* had been launched. It predictably matured during the run, gaining strength from the response of audiences which steadily increased in capacity and appreciation of the work. (7)

There is a sense in which a new play is never finished. The point at which a performance occurs isn't the point at which perfection has been reached. It is simply the stage at which the production group are ready/forced to share the experience of a play with an audience. Work on a production doesn't stop. It continues in a different form and *Landmark* was no exception to this. The first performance was flat, but others later in the week, when we had adjusted to the presence of an audience and recognised their unpredictability, went extremely well. It was never predictable. But then, why should it be? Live theatre is about live responses to live actors. It is through that very unpredictability that one learns how long to pause, effective timing, delivering and picking up on cues, audibility, physical response, energy levels, convincing motivation, credible characterisation. One learns by feeling the audience's response; by listening to them responding. They are the last link in the circle begun by the writer, evolved by the director, developed by the actors, visualised by the designer and realised by the production crew. In six nights of performances we managed six versions of *Landmark*. The text remains for others, perhaps, to continue the process. (4)

THE PROJECT

The advantage of working in a University theatre is that experiments can be made; the actors are not looking to the production as a means of obtaining the next job. What is much more important is the process as a means of learning about theatre. Being part of a production team reminds you that play-texts are shells. Unlike novels they do not exist in their own right and need the resources of a group of people working together in order to make them live at all. (4)

(1) Ed O'Regan
(2) Wanda Zyborska
(3) Martin Pudney
(4) Ruth Shade
(5) Leslie Bell
(6) Nicolle Freni
(7) Charles Butler

LANDMARK

a play by Steve Gooch

(formerly 'Our Land, Our Lives')

The play is set in 1980 and takes place in a barn. There are six scenes, preferably in three acts.

CHARACTERS

    CAROL
    SANDY
    GARY
    JIM
    DI
    DON

    GEORGE
    TED
    JOYCE KNIGHT   } Some doubling
    LES   of these characters is possible

    TV DIRECTOR
    TV TECHNICIAN

SONG

Growing, growing, growing, gone
You and me and everyone
Growing, growing, growing, gone
Our lives are over before they're begun.

    They tell us growth's a good thing
    On that they all agree
    But what they grow is for themselves
    And not for you and me.

Growing, growing, etc.

    As kids we're full of fancies
    We never see the snags
    And by the time we're thirty
    Our hopes all hang in rags.

Growing, growing, etc.

SCENE I

The barn. Late summer evening.
Bales of straw, farm implements and machinery, packing-cases, oil-drums, etc. Bags of chemicals lean against one wall.
A voice outside.

CAROL   Shine the torch.

CAROL *unlocks the barn door and pushes it wide as she comes in. Blue light from outside.* **SANDY** *comes in, carrying a torch.*

SANDY	Dear me.
CAROL	Bring back memories?
SANDY	I don't dare think.
CAROL	Well we had to have a last look. — If I can find the light.
SANDY	Only you could think of this, Carol.
CAROL	What d'you mean by that!
SANDY	I mean, it's a lovely idea.
CAROL	You're as bad as Di. First thing she said when I phoned her: 'Lovely idea. Let's get a campaign goin'.'
SANDY	It is a shame they're pullin' it down.
CAROL	Why she can't just have a bit of fun an' leave it at that, I don't know.
SANDY	She always was the serious one.
CAROL	Bloody wet-blanket, you ask me. *(Finds the switch)* There.
SANDY	Well I say!
CAROL	Glad you came?
SANDY	It's funny. It all looks different, but it feels the same. — How'd you get the key?
CAROL	Old George. Remember him?
SANDY	He doesn't still work here!
CAROL	Odd jobs now, that's all.
SANDY	How'd you meet up with him again?
CAROL	Comes in the pub every Tuesday. After he's picked up his pension.

GARY *and* **JIM** *approach from outside.*

GARY	Is this it then?
CAROL	What'd you expect, the Corn Market?

Scene I

GARY	*(Coming in)* I remembered it bigger, that's all.
CAROL	Course you would. How old were we?
SANDY	Thirteen?
JIM	*(Comes in carrying a 6-pack of beer)* Well, well, well.
CAROL	Hasn't changed much, has it.
SANDY	Unlike us.
GARY	*They* were never here before.
SANDY	What?
GARY	Them chemicals.
JIM	You're not startin' that again?
CAROL	You two been settin' the world to rights?
JIM	He has.
SANDY	What are they for anyway?
GARY	Oh, they got all kinds of good uses. *(Smiles)* There's one kind for killin' things off. Another for growin' em again after you used the first kind. Then there's another to compensate for not lettin' nature take her course in the first place.
JIM	Suppose you think the wheel was a big mistake an' all.
GARY	Depends what it's on, Jim.

DI *comes in, followed by* **DON**

DI	Well I never.
DON	Stone me.
SANDY	Takes you back, don't it.
DON	Just as well we had a drink first.
JIM	Shock too much for you, Don?
DON	*(Laughs)* I feel like a drownin' man. Past rushin' before my eyes.
CAROL	Maybe you *shouldn't* have had that drink first.
DON	I could do with another now, I can tell you.
SANDY	Well I think it was a good idea of Carol's.
DON	Absolutely. Vote of thanks all round.
CAROL	It wasn't only me. We sort of thought of it together, didn't we, Jim.
JIM	She did all the work, mind.
DON	That figures. *(To* **GARY***)* Area Manager now, you know.
CAROL	No, fair's fair. We all did our bit. Di found Sandy. An' you found Gary.
DON	What did Management do?
CAROL	Well he's a busy man now, aren't you Jim.
JIM	Keeps me off the streets, I suppose.
DON	Not too busy for a nostalgic executive lunch in the Royal Oak though, obviously.
JIM	Well if the landlady insists!

DI	You still do your singin' there, Carol?
CAROL	*(Quiet)* No.
JIM	You do. Occasionally. For a special do.
CAROL	Not really.
DI	Shame.

Pause.

SANDY	What happened, Carol?
CAROL	*(After a pause)* I gave it up. *(Pause)* Eddie said we needed other attractions. I knew what that meant. Well I mean, my singin' helped him get that place goin'. Anyway, I went over to the competition. Singin' round the 'Sun'. Caused quite a stir at the time.
DI	I can imagine!
CAROL	Yeh well, same story there in the end. So I tried the clubs for a while.
DI	What was that like?
CAROL	Awful. Grabbin' agents, lechy club managers, doin' the rounds all the time . . . felt like 'Pass the Parcel'. 'Cept I'd never exactly fancied myself gift-wrapped. So I went crawlin' back to Eddie. No more singin' though.
DI	Shame.

Pause.

DON	*(To **JIM**)* You just goin' a stand holdin' them cans or what?
CAROL	Well we know who's turned out an alcoholic anyway.
DON	Only for a toast. We got to have a toast!
CAROL	We've had three already.
DON	Not in situ though. At the scene of the crime. — There anythin' to sit on?
GARY	Here.

They arrange an impromptu table and chairs.

CAROL	Might've known he'd start organisin' us.
SANDY	Just like the old days.
JIM	Be signin' us up for the Union next.
DON	Not you, mate. Even if I though there was a glimmer of a chance, I'd still hesitate.
CAROL	That's enough, you two. — Where's them crisps?
DON	Least I ain't the only one with an addiction.
CAROL	Give over!
GARY	What was it we used to call Carol?

Scene I

CAROL	Dustbin.
JIM	Di was Worm.
SANDY	An' I was Mouse.
CAROL	Proper little gentlemen, weren't they Sandy.
SANDY	An' they ain't changed.
DI	A bit fatter round the middle maybe?
SANDY	Bit taller in the forehead?
CAROL	Well I don't care. More mouths to feed in the world, less food to go round. I'm gettin' mine now while the goin's good. *(Starts on crisps)*
GARY	That's not true, you know.
CAROL	What?
GARY	Less food. The resources are there. It's just the way they're channelled.
JIM	*(To CAROL)* Nature Boy's at it again.
DI	Least one of us kept close to the land.
GARY	Chance'd be a fine thing. This place says it all. If we're not financiers or chemists these days, we're bloody motor mechanics.
JIM	Good thing too. If you want better yields.
GARY	In the short-term maybe. But what are we doin' to the soil meanwhile?
CAROL	Honestly! We've hardly been together five minutes an' they're at it. *(To DI)* They haven't changed, have they.
DON	Course they have. Like the price a crisps. — May I? *(He pinches a crisp from CAROL)*
CAROL	Get your own!
SANDY	Threepence a bag they used to be.
DI	Eggs one an' six a half dozen.
SANDY	Cheese two bob a pound.
GARY	That's only when we were kids. What about our grandparents?
SANDY	Terrifyin' when you think.
DON	You mean you do occasionally?
GARY	It's how we measure the years these days, inflation.
DON	Those who have wantin' more, so those who want havin' to pay more.
JIM	Very profound.
DON	I suppose you put it all down to wages.
JIM	They help.
GARY	Not mine, mate. Agricultural worker's still the lowest paid in the country. Don't stop the price a sugar an' potatoes soarin' through the roof.
DON	Half a crown pocket money I used to get. 12½p!
DI	An' we'd sit round like this an' share out what we bought. Remember?

CAROL	I'd save a month to buy a forty-five. Duane Eddy Number One!

Music.

DI	What was it you used to say?
DON	I declare another extraordinary General Meeting . . .
SANDY	I *hereby* declare another extraordinar*ily* General Meeting.
DON	Total bloody recall, this one.

Music. The Gang as teenagers. Light change.

DON	Right then. I hereby declare another Extraordinarily General Meetin' of the Red Mouth Gang open. One, two, three, four, five — who's not here?
JIM	Worm.
DON	Why not?
GARY	Late.
DON	She can't be.
GARY	Is though.
DON	Can't be! If this is a proper gang, we got to have proper discipline.
SANDY	It's her Mum an' Dad. They make her do the washin'-up after tea.
DON	Why?
SANDY	They say they're too tired. *(Confidential, to* **CAROL***)* Her Mum works, you know.
CAROL	Really?
DON	What difference's that make? My Mum works. She ain't too tired.
CAROL	It's not her place to. A woman's place is in the home.
DON	My Dad says it's good for her.
JIM	He would.
SANDY	Your Mum works cos your Dad don't earn enough to keep you, cos he's always off at strikes an' things.
DON	He's not always off at strikes an' things! You don't understand nothin'!
JIM	Order! Order!
DON	You can't call order. I'm the one calls order cos I'm in the chair. *(Pause)* Order.
GARY	*(Suddenly stands)* Death to all Mums an' Dads!
DON	You can't call for that. It's not on the agenda.
SANDY	Good idea though.
GARY	An' teachers!
CAROL	Yeh, an' teachers. Write it in the Gang Book.

CAROL *writes.* **DI** *comes in.*

Scene I

DI	Sorry. I had to do the washin'-up.
JIM	This is stupid. You can't have meetings an' people turnin' up late. An' you can't write 'Death to all Mums an' Dads' if you got no way of killin' em.
SANDY	It's just a nice idea.
JIM	To kill someone you got to have a gun or a knife. You ain't got none of them things. Anyway, I don't want to kill my Mum an' Dad.
GARY	Why not?
JIM	I quite like 'em. Anyway, if you killed your Mum an' Dad, who'd give you your pocket money?
CAROL	Er.
DI	She could go to work.
GARY	Yeh!
CAROL	I wouldn't though. I'd have a man to keep me.
DON	We're gettin' off the subject. We come here tonight for a reason. To swear the Oath of Brotherhood.
DI	What about us? The girls. We ain't brothers.
GARY	You were late.
DI	What do *we* swear?
DON	The Oath of Sisterhood.
SANDY	No, it's got to be the same.
DON	What d'you mean?
SANDY	What the boys swear's got to be the same as what the girls swear.
JIM	It is the same. Just a different name.
DON	All right. The Oath of the Red Mouth Gang. How's that?
CAROL	All right.
DON	Now what we do, we all cut our thumbs an' mingle our blood.
SANDY	Eurgh!
CAROL	I ain't doin' that.
DON	We got to if we want to be blood bro--- *(Realises)* Oh.
CAROL	I ain't cuttin' my thumb. Not for no-one.
DI	It's only a little nick. No worse'n when you stick a pin in sewin'.
CAROL	I don't mind doin' it by accident, but not on purpose.
DON	Come on, it won't hurt.
CAROL	Course it will. What you take me for?
SANDY	I vote the girls don't have to if they don't want to.
DON	There's no point if you don't do it.
CAROL	We can mingle in your blood. Almost as good.
DON	It's not the same. It was you wanted to be the same, wasn't it?
SANDY	Yeh, but it's your idea.

GARY	I ain't doin' it if the girls ain't doin' it.
DON	There! *(He cuts his thumb)*
SANDY	Eurgh!
DON	Come on, Jim.

JIM cuts his thumb.

Gary.

Reluctantly, **GARY** *cuts his thumb.*

GARY	Ow!
DI	I'm next. *(She does it)*
DON	If she can do it, you two can.
CAROL	No, I ain't.
SANDY	Me neither.
DI	Go on, it's easy.
CAROL	No.
JIM	It don't hurt.
CAROL	No!!
GARY	Sandy?
SANDY	I'm scared.
DON	All right, girls are excused. Now press 'em together. Everyone with everyone else.

They do this.

Now we're a real gang.

SONG

We've been through the hoop
We've done it together
We're a gang, we're a group
We'll go on for ever.

We live in the same town
We're all the same age
Our Mums get the same housekeepin'
Our Dads get the same wage.

We're in the same school
With the same schoolteachers
Where the same headmaster
Makes the same old speeches

We play the same games
In the road an' on the grass
We're not just a gang
We're a class.

Scene I

Back as adults.

JIM	Proper little tyrant, wasn't he.
CAROL	Barbarian, more like. All that blood-lettin'.
GARY	The real barbarians are down the road. D'you see as we come along? More army bases round here now than farmhouses.
DI	I thought you were in the army once?
GARY	That's how I know what I'm talkin' about.
DI	Don't seem like you.
GARY	Remember I always wanted to go to Australia? Sheep-shearin'. Well, I couldn't get there any other way, so I thought I'd try that one. Germany was as far as I got.
DON	Come out, become a hippy.
CAROL	Gary a hippy!
GARY	Yeh, in London.
DON	From the sublime to the ridiculous.
GARY	Least they had the army sussed. Bloody discipline an' all that.
JIM	Don knows all about discipline, don't you Don.
DON	Leave it out, will you?
JIM	District Secretary, now is it?
CAROL	Now come on, don't you two start again. I didn't get us here to quarrel.
DI	Why did you get us here, Carol?
CAROL	Not for what you think either.
DI	What then?
CAROL	Well, I just thought . . . it's twenty years since we sat in here an' cut our thumbs. When I heard they were pullin' the old place down, I just thought it'd be nice to get together again. Have a few drinks, chat about old times. Turns out Di wants to make a bloody public issue of it.
DI	Well it is a scandal what they're doin' to this area.
GARY	Too damn right.
SANDY	Why are they pullin' it down anyway?
GARY	My guess is carrots.
CAROL	I beg your pardon!
GARY	They got this new system for growin' 'em now, you see. Keep the seed under glass till it sprouts, coat it in a nutrient jelly, then plop each unit whole in the ground from a special machine. Every one a winner.
CAROL	Good for them.
DON	'Cept they also try an' get 'em all the same size. So they fit in the cans.
SANDY	Oh no! *(She laughs)*

GARY   What's so funny?
SANDY   It's just the thought of it. All them little shoots in their little holes. Then in their little cans. *(Laughs on)*
GARY   Biggest joke is, it ain't cost-effective 'less the machine's got a clear 18-acre run.
DI   An' our old barn's in the way?
GARY   That's my guess. *(He glances at **JIM**)*
DI   Not just the barn. Old George's cottage too.
GARY   He's not still around?
DI   We're dealin' with his case at our office. It's a tied cottage.
GARY   He's still workin' then?
CAROL   Redundant. Year before last.
SANDY   We were always warnin' him that would happen.
CAROL   Bloody little know-alls.
SANDY   Only cos we hated it here so much.
CAROL   Yeh well, he lasted longer'n we did.
SANDY   An' now this.

> *Pause.*

DON   I thought they passed legislation on tied cottages.
DI   They did. But makin' it stick's another matter.
SANDY   He's lived there all his life though!
DI   The farmer only kept him on there as a favour.
GARY   Won't the Council rehouse him?
DI   It's not up to them in the first instance. *(Pause. She looks at **JIM**)* It's up to the purchaser. *(Pause)* Your firm, Jim.
JIM   Sorry?
DI   Didn't you know?
JIM   Who you been dealin' with?
DI   London.
JIM   Oh well, they don't tell us nothin'.
DI   Will it come to you?
JIM   Could do.
SANDY   Maybe you can help them?

> **JIM** *doesn't answer.*

CAROL   Listen, I really think —
SANDY   There must be something we can do. *(To **DI**)* I mean, if your firm are solicitors . . .
DI   We're doin' what we can. But it takes time.
SANDY   An' what'll happen to him otherwise?
DI   Old folks' home?
SANDY   That's terrible. *(To **CAROL**)* You didn't tell me this.

Scene I

CAROL   I didn't know.

Pause. **JIM** *gets up.*

CAROL   *(Quick)* Listen, maybe we ought to talk about somethin' else.
JIM   It's all right, Carol. Just takin' the dog for a walk.
DON   Mine'll need one too in a minute. *(Reaches for another can)*
CAROL   Here, take the torch.

JIM *takes it and goes out.*

DON   Awkward, en it.
GARY   Maybe he could help.
DON   Doin' what? Puttin' his job on the line?
CAROL   I think we ought to forget about it for now, don't you? I mean, we don't want to spoil our evenin'.
DON   Yeh. No point frettin' over somethin' that might not happen.

Pause.

GARY   Trust old George to stick a spanner in the works.
CAROL   He never let on to me, you know.
GARY   Never let on about anythin', old George.
CAROL   Just as well, with all that used to go on in here.
DON   That's right. Who's for a cuddle then? *(Goes to cuddle* **CAROL***)*
CAROL   Really, Don! You're a married man, now.
DON   So what? You're a married woman.
CAROL   Get off! — Anyway, it wasn't me you used to fancy.
DON   You sure?
SANDY   Went for anythin' and everythin', he did.
CAROL   Oh, thanks very much.
SANDY   I'm includin' me!
DI   I don't remember all this.
GARY   Your Mum wouldn't let you out.
DI   Of course.
SANDY   Gary was just as bad.
CAROL   I always thought he was the shy one.
SANDY   Only in comparison.
DON   Oh?
SANDY   That's as much as I'm sayin'.

Pause.

DI   D'you think Jim's all right?

DON	Worried he's run off?
DI	I'll see what he's up to.
DON	He has had four pints, don't forget.
CAROL	You won't say nothin'?
DI	Don't worry.
CAROL	Promise?
DON	*(To* **DI***)* If you scream, we'll know it's indecent exposure.
CAROL	Really, Don! *(To others)* En 'e awful.
DON	It's all this back to nature talk. Takes me like that.
SANDY	Basically they don't grow up, do they. Men.
CAROL	Well, some of 'em *(She glances at* **GARY***)*
DON	Aye-aye! I saw that! Wanna change places, Gary?
GARY	Sit down.
SANDY	See? He's still shy, basically.
GARY	What about you two? Giggly as ever.
SANDY	I'm not normally. It's just meetin' up again.
CAROL	Funny, en it. You sort of slip into old ways.
GARY	You're tellin' me. I remember one time . . .
SANDY	So do I.

Music. Light change. **DON** *and* **GARY**, **CAROL** *and* **SANDY** *as teenagers.*

GARY	Oh go on.
SANDY	No.
GARY	It's good fun. It's not just motor-bikes. They have clowns an' things. And you can get hot-dogs if you like. An' pepsis.
SANDY	I ain' interested though. It's a bore, speedway.
CAROL	'Sides, why should we wanna go with a coupla scruffs like you?
DON	Bloody snob!
CAROL	Well look at you! Hair all over the place, tatty jeans, never wear a tie.
DON	Why should we? Have to wear 'em at school all the time.
CAROL	Suppose you want us to go Dutch too.
GARY	What's that mean?
DON	Well, we'd expect you to chip in. Of course.
SANDY	Plenty of blokes in this town take us out in suits. An' won't let us pay for nothin'.
GARY	So?
SANDY	So nothin'. I'm just tell' you.
GARY	Yeh but they go to work. I mean, they're older.
CAROL	Mature, that's all.
GARY	What d'you mean, mature?
SANDY	Everyone knows girls mature faster'n boys.

Scene I

CAROL	Girl's got to be careful with you men. You're all the same. Spend hours gettin' a girl where you want her, then forget about it completely after.
DON	Your fault if you get a bloke goin'.
SANDY	Us who have to live with the consequences though.
DON	We know that! Got kitted out before we came.
CAROL	Yeh?
DON	Show her, Gary.
GARY	See? Three an' nine for three.
CAROL	Between the two of you? Who's goin' twice?
DON	Thought we'd share that one.

The girls splutter.

CAROL	Typical!
GARY	We ain't made of money!
CAROL	So I've noticed.
DON	Sshh.
CAROL	Sshh yourself.
DON	No, someone outside.
GARY	Not them big blokes again. On bikes.
CAROL	He's scared!
DON	Might be the law.
SANDY	Probably just old George.

A knock.

GEORGE	*(Off)* Can I come in?
SANDY	Told you.
DON	Yeh, come in, George.

GEORGE *comes in. He carries a stove and a brown paper bag.*

GEORGE	Thought you might be cold. Winter comin' on.
CAROL	Thanks, George. — En he kind.
GEORGE	Few apples. In the orchard this mornin'. Late un's. Cut the bits out, they'll be all right.
SANDY	*(Taking them)* Eurgh, not maggoty, are they? I don't like maggoty apples.
GARY	Don't be so fussy.
DON	Thanks, George.
GEORGE	Should be enough paraffin in there. If it runs out, let me know.
GARY	Yeh.

GEORGE	An' don't get stayin' out late now it's nice an' warm. Have your mums an' dads after me. *(Goes to go)*
DON	It true your mate Arthur's leavin' the farm?
GEORGE	Who told you that?
DON	My Dad. He said there weren't enough work for him.
GEORGE	Yeh well, he's gettin' on, old Arthur.

The girls giggle.

GARY	Ain't much younger yourself, George.
GEORGE	I been with Mr Frankland longer though.
DON	So?
GEORGE	Well someone's got to go, ain't they.
DON	Cos of the machines?
GEORGE	What machines?
DON	My Dad says it's cos they're gettin' machines now to do the work of men.
GEORGE	That's part of it, yeh.
DON	Well, that's not fair. Who you goin' to have to talk to?
GEORGE	Arthur an' me never talked much anyway. 'Sides, can't stand in the way of progress. Machines do it faster'n men. Cheaper. If it's makin' food for everyone, that's all to the good, ain't it?
DON	Suppose so.
GEORGE	Tried fightin' the machines when my Grandad was a boy. Didn't do 'em no good. Still came in the end. One day it'll all be machines, I dare say.

Pause. The kids aren't convinced.

	Come round Saturday afternoon. I'll show you the new beet harvester. That's a beauty. All right?
DON	Yeh.
GARY	Can I come too?
GEORGE	Course. Don't be too late tonight now. *(Goes)*
CAROL	Just sits an' lets it happen to him. Stupid!
DON	It's cos the farmworkers' union ain't strong, my Dad says.
CAROL	Unions! It's cos he wants to wake up!
GARY	What can he do though?
CAROL	I know what I'd do.
GARY	What?

Pause.

CAROL	Somethin', any rate. I wouldn't get stuck in a dead end like this.

Scene I

SONG

The people who know how to share
The people who know how to care
Are the people the hard ones break
The people from whom they take.

> For when you're working together
> Scraping by together
> The other man's problem
> Becomes your problem too;
> But when it's dog eats dog
> The one that gets eaten
> Is the one who understands
> The other's point of view.

So the people who know how to share
The people who know how to care
Become the people the hard ones break
The people from whom they take.

Back as adults.

DON	Did get stuck though, didn't we.
CAROL	Not all of us. Sandy moved away. An' Gary's workin' in Lincolnshire.

DI *and* **JIM** *come back in.*

SANDY	Hardly Australia though, is it.
CAROL	Just as well. Never've got hold of you there.
DON	*(To* **DI***)* How'd you find her?
DI	County Library.
GARY	Jack Jones here found me through the Union. Couldn't believe it when I opened the letter. After the army an' London. Thought I'd left all this behind me.
JIM	Big Brother, eh.
DON	Least we don't run files on people's credit-worthiness.
JIM	Got to know where you stand with people, Don.
DON	*(To* **DI***)* Do we know where we stand with him?
DI	We didn't talk about it.
CAROL	*(In quick)* What I want to know is, what everyone's been doin' with 'emselves.
DON	Yeh. I never did find out why you moved, Sandy.
CAROL	See? It *was* her he was sweet on.
SANDY	Honestly, Carol. — No, there was no special reason. Mum an' Dad just wanted to get out of the area.

DON	Away from our bad influence, I suppose.
SANDY	That's not far off the truth.
CAROL	You're jokin'.
SANDY	Oh no. Mum was always goin' on about us 'betterin' ourselves'.
CAROL	She never came on snobby with me.
SANDY	No, she was always nice to everyone. To their faces.
CAROL	Oh.
DI	She'll be well pleased now then.
SANDY	Actually, she's dead now.
DI	Oh I'm sorry.
SANDY	It's all right. Saw me married an' settled before she went. That was all she cared about.

Pause.

CAROL	Well it is nice where you are.
SANDY	Oh yes. Nice little house, nice little garden, two nice kids an' a nice civil servant for a husband.

Slight pause. The others embarrassed.

CAROL	Steady though, eh.
SANDY	Oh yeh, it's steady all right. Can't say it ain't steady.

Pause again.

I'm stuck there really. You know? Keepin' the mantelpiece clear, wipin' finger-marks off the light-switch. Tops of the doors. Sometimes I feel I've got so much pressure inside me, if I don't let it out, I'll explode. *(Pause)* Not at the kids though. I don't see why they should suffer. But I won't pretend. Like my Mum did. That everything's hunkey-dorey. Do more harm makin' the best of a bad job than you do chuckin' it. *(Pause)* Not that anyone knows about all this, mind. I just potter on in my own quiet way. *(Pause)* Oh yes, it's certainly steady.

Pause.

CAROL	That can be worth a lot. I wouldn't mind things a bit quieter.
DON	You? You wouldn't know what to do with yourself.
CAROL	No? I can think of plenty of things.
DON	Oh come on, Carol. You love that pub. All the gossip, the company.

Scene I

DI	You don't get much of a home life, Don, runnin' a pub.
CAROL	That's just it. The pub *is* our home. Not that Eddie does much around it.
JIM	He's a good landlord.
CAROL	To the customers maybe.

Pause. Now it's her turn.

We just don't get any time to ourselves. You know? I mean, Eddie an' me never talked about me goin' off. Just took me back like I'd gone the day before. You get caught in a sort of treadmill, don't you. Habit. Just copin'. No time to sit an' relax. Reflect.

Pause.

DON	Jim of course does nothin' else these days.
DI	He certainly seems well settled.
JIM	Yeh. Can't complain.

Pause. He's not going to enlarge.

DON	Why should he? Stuck in the rat-race. Promotion every two years. Beats workin' for a livin'.
JIM	That why you keep makin' snide remarks about it?
DON	Me? I'm happy as a sandboy. Fulfilled in life.
GARY	Given the still outstandin' overthrow of capitalism.
DON	We all have our crosses.
DI	Sounded earlier like you were the rebel, Gary.
GARY	No. I don't like what they're doin' to the land. But I just keep me head down an' get on with it. Had enough of politics in London.

Pause. The others wait.

We were squattin' this big house. You know? Share an' share alike. Only I seemed to be the only one workin', so I was doin' all the sharin'. Never found out what the others did — 'cept zoom home to their rich parents every other weekend. Didn't share none of that of course. Just their indignation. I decided if I was goin' a be on my own, I might as well do it without company. *(Pause)* One thing about farm work. You can keep yourself to yourself if you want.

CAROL	See, *he* gets time to think.
GARY	Too much sometimes.

17

DI	You work on your own then?
GARY	Most of us do now. One man, ten machines.
DON	Professional hermits.
CAROL	His own best company, aren't you Gary.
DON	Terrific. Employ the solitary types, stops 'em gettin' organised.
CAROL	Honestly, Don. *(To others)* Never happy 'less he's havin' a go at someone.
SANDY	Yeh, what about you, Don? Who'd you marry?
CAROL	That's what she really wants to know!
SANDY	Oh shut up, Carol *(Pause)* Well?
DON	You wouldn't know her. Lesley. Good wife. An' mother.

Pause. They wait for him to enlarge.

	Intelligent woman.
CAROL	'Cept he never sees her.
DI	Too many meetings.
DON	Yeh well, someone's got to do it.

Pause.

CAROL	Remember the Oath?
DI	Oh no!
GARY	Which one?
CAROL	Never to grow up like our parents.
SANDY	Oh God.
JIM	I was wonderin' when that'd come up.
CAROL	I think Don still wants to live it out.
DON	An' why not! We had somethin' as kids. What we said an' did went together.
JIM	What d'you expect? We've grown up, that's all.
DON	Growin' up don't have to mean givin' up, you know.
JIM	Earnin' your living, payin' the rent . . . none of that's real when you're thirteen. You're out of it all.
GARY	An' now?
DON	We're out of joint. With ourselves.
JIM	I don't believe we were ever in.
DON	You weren't.
JIM	What d'you mean?
DON	You never took the Oath in the first place. Remember?
DI	I do. Vaguely.

As teenagers. Music. Light change.

JIM	It's impossible.

Scene I

CAROL	Nothin's impossible till you try.
JIM	This is. How we goin' a tell?
DI	What d'you mean?
JIM	We got to wait till we're the same age.
DON	That's not difficult.
JIM	So that's one way we're goin' a be like 'em for a start.
SANDY	How?
JIM	The same age!
SANDY	Oh.
JIM	An' anyway, how we goin' a meet up? Could be anywhere by then. Gary wants to go to Australia.
CAROL	Sheep-shearin'. Believe that when I see it.
GARY	Just you wait!
SANDY	It's only because we're breakin' up, Jim.
CAROL	Yeh, if we're goin' out, we wanna go out with a bang. Somethin' to remember.
JIM	Remember! We'll have it hangin' over our heads for the rest of our lives.
DON	That's the idea. Stop us gettin' like . . . Them.
JIM	No chance. I mean, we're all goin' that way already.
SANDY	Who is?
JIM	Well you are for a kick-off.
SANDY	I am not!
JIM	Mum's apron on when you help in the kitchen. Borrowin' her shoes. I've seen you.
SANDY	Yeh, but I ain't the same.
JIM	You will be.
DI	*(To* **JIM***)* Reason you don't wanna do it, you're too much like your old man already.
JIM	I ain't!
DI	His bloody echo, you are.
JIM	Never!
DI	Even bloody look like him.
JIM	I don't. *(Pause)* He's got hairs up his nose.
DON	How we goin' a do this then?
JIM	You're determined, aren't you. If you say it's gotta be done, everyone says it.
GARY	He ain't the only one.
JIM	Well, I ain't goin' a do it.
DI	We haven't said what we're doin' yet.
SANDY	Not minglin' blood, I hope. I couldn't stand that again.
CAROL	No, it's got to be different, this. Permanent. We got to feel it'll always be there.
DON	Bury somethin'.
GARY	What d'you mean?

DON	Our badges, the Gang Book... somethin' else. Put it all in the tin an' bury it. The Gang's dead so we bury it.
DI	That's not much though, is it. Just the badges an' the book. It's got to be somethin' we remember.
GARY	It's got to hurt. If it don't hurt we won't remember it.
SANDY	A lock of hair.
CAROL	Oh no! I just had mine done!
GARY	That hurts, that's good.
DON	An' money. Sixpence each.
JIM	It's ridiculous. A waste. Be three bob in there.
GARY	He's right. 'Sides, I ain't got sixpence.
DON	Whatever you got then.
GARY	I ain't got nothin'. Spent it all. I don't get as much as the rest of you.
DON	You must have somethin'. Empty your pockets.
SANDY	I got some scissors.
DON	Great. Get crackin'.

SANDY *starts cutting hair.*

JIM	This is stupid.
DON	*(To* **JIM***)* Sixpence please. In the tin.
JIM	I'm goin'.
DON	*(To* **CAROL***)* Sixpence please. *(Gets it, moves on)*
JIM	Listen, if this is all it's goin' a be, I don't wanna know. I'd sooner just let it . . . fade.

DI *gives* **DON** *sixpence.* **SANDY** *cuts* **GARY***'s hair.*

DON	What you got?
GARY	Chewin'-gum.
DON	That'll do. Put it in.
SANDY	Come on, Miss Teazie-Weazie, you're next.
CAROL	He's got a point, you know. It's a bit . . . nothin', en it.
DON	*(To* **SANDY***)* Do me. *(* **SANDY** *cuts his hair)* Sixpence in. *(* **SANDY** *puts sixpence in)*
DI	Come on, me next.
JIM	Listen, I don't wanna go without... well you know, it's been a long time . . . but it's childish, this . . . this ain't what it's about.
GARY	Fuck off.
JIM	I just think there ought to be somethin' else.
CAROL	Come on then.*(* **SANDY** *cuts her hair)*
JIM	Be seein' you then.

Scene I

DON	Cheers.
CAROL	Cheers, Jim.
DI	Tat-ta.

    JIM *goes.*

SANDY   Now me.

    CAROL *cuts her hair and pops it in the tin.*

DON	Find a good place, dig it in, an' that's it. Never forget it.
SANDY	No.

    SONG

    Getting older
    We have to shoulder
    The weight we see
    Bend others' knees
    We have to find
    A clause that binds
    Makes what we feel
    A strength that's real.

      It's got to count
      It's got to mean something
      Got to hurt
      Not slip away
      It's got to bite
      If we're to do something
      Got to tell
      If we're to have our say.

    Yes, it must count etc.

    Back as adults.

DON	See? He was lettin' the side down even then.
JIM	Exactly who's lettin' who down remains to be seen, comrade.
DON	The proof, friend, is in history.
JIM	I look forward, Don, not back.
DON	Scared a what you might see over your shoulder?
CAROL	Now come on, Don. I've said it enough times. *(To the others)* Bloody unions.
DON	Contrary to popular belief, Carol, it's not us who are holdin' the country to ransom.

JIM	Don't tell me, it's us, the big bad multinationals.
DON	Supranationals.
JIM	Oh 'supra' are we now? That's a new one.
DON	Above and beyond our control, that's why.
JIM	We work within the law, Don. Same as most people.
DON	Till you wanna change it.
JIM	We've all got an equal, democratic right to do that.
DON	But that kinda democracy, Jim, comes easier with a few million dollars behind you.
JIM	*(Finishing his drink)* It's gettin' late.
CAROL	You're not goin'?
JIM	Got to, I'm afraid. Joan'll be waitin' up.
CAROL	*(To DON)* You're goin' a drive him off now like you did then.
DON	Why blame me!
JIM	Quite right. Don't make him out more important than he is.
SANDY	You were right, Carol. They are still at it.
CAROL	*(Of DON)* He's like his old man, for one.
GARY	I got a feelin' we all are. Let ourselves get caught out.
JIM	Yeh well, some of us may've moved on. *(Gets up)*
DON	What to though?
DI	Why *didn't* you join in, Jim?
JIM	Maybe I was just gettin' too old for it all. Even then.
DON	'Ark at Father Time!
JIM	I'd better be goin' *(Finds his coat and begins putting it on)*
CAROL	*(To DON)* See what you've done.
DON	I tell you, if we had one ounce a the rebellion we had as kids, one ounce a the solidarity —
JIM	It's all in your head, Don.
DON	Pullin' this place down, is that in my head?
CAROL	Don!
DON	What do we do then? Just let 'em get away with it?
DI	That's right. We never did talk about George's cottage.
CAROL	Di, you promised!
JIM	Listen, I've seen the way this evenin's been goin' . . .
DON	Oh? What way's that?
JIM	It was supposed to be a friendly reunion, right? A few drinks an' a bit a nostalgia. But instead it's turnin' into somethin' else.
DON	What exactly?
JIM	I don't know, but I don't want no part of it.
GARY	I'm enjoyin' it. Cards on the table. Skeletons out the cupboard. It's a breath of fresh air.
DON	That's right. No sense bein' intimidated by what you don't know.

Scene I

JIM	I ain' intimidated.
DON	Behavin' like it.
JIM	You can carry on if you like . . .
DON	We will.
JIM	It's been really nice, Carol. Lovely idea. Thanks.
CAROL	*(Getting up)* D'you have to go?
JIM	Maybe another time. — I will look into this business with George, Di. I'll let you know.
CAROL	Can you find your way?
JIM	Cheers, everyone. All the best.
CAROL	I'll bring the torch. *(She goes with **JIM**)*
SANDY	Oh dear.
DI	Well it had to be said. Start losin' people now, we'll never get anything off the ground.
SANDY	Like what?
GARY	Yeh, what *are* you two up to?
DI	It's no big secret. Just an idea we had on the way over. I'd like to get some sort of protest goin'.
GARY	You'll have problems if Jim's firm's involved.
DON	Not least with Carol.
SANDY	It does seem a shame though.
DI	Shame? It's a bloody scandal!
CAROL	*(Coming back in)* You an' your big mouth!
DON	What did I say?
CAROL	Him or you, it always was. Always competin'.
DON	I hardly opened me mouth!
CAROL	You don't have to. Just bein' there's enough.
DON	I'm sorry! If I could dissolve into thin air, I would!
DI	We had to find out, Carol.
CAROL	Find out what?
DI	Well, if we're goin' to do somethin' about this place . . .
CAROL	Who said we are?
DI	Well I'm serious about it.
CAROL	I've had enough of this. Just gettin' nice an' cosy . . . It's only an ol' barn for Christ's sake!
DI	It isn't only this place, Carol. It's George's cottage, what Gary was talkin' about, the agribusiness. It's squeezin' out a whole way of life.
DON	Thing is, you see Carol, it's the Rally next week.
	Pause.
CAROL	Jim was right. You are up to something.
DI	It's no great conspiracy, Carol. Honestly. No big deal.
GARY	You can say that again. The Rally's a bloody farce these days. Not a patch on what it used to be.

DON	It celebrates the beginnings of your union, friend. The victims of the Great Lock-Out.
DI	*(Looking at* **CAROL***)* We just thought . . . a stall or something.
CAROL	I see. Bein' shanghaied into the People's Army, are we. I didn't come here for this. *(Picks up her things)*
SANDY	Carol. At least you could hear them out.

CAROL, *feeling betrayed, looks at her.*

GARY	Mind you, you'll need more'n just a stall to make an impression on the Rally these days. It's all big companies showin' off their new products.
DON	Just have to outgun 'em then.
GARY	What with? You an' a water-pistol?
DON	*(Not without irony)* The people's resources, brother, are infinite. We got the biggest star in the county right here.

They turn towards **CAROL**, *who is putting on her coat.*

CAROL	Jesus Christ, you've got a nerve! Comin' here, ruinin' our evening... after all our hard work... then you got the barefaced — I'll leave the key with you, Sandy. Do what you like. *(She goes to the door)*
SANDY	Carol.
CAROL	You comin'?
SANDY	Er . . . *(Looks at the others)*
CAROL	See you then. *(Goes)*
SANDY	I'd better talk to her. *(She slips her coat on and follows Carol)*
DI	Done it again, Don.
GARY	Subtlety personified.
DON	I wasn't goin' a take all that lyin' down.
DI	Coulda tried forcin' yourself for once.
DON	What's that supposed to mean?
DI	You just wind yourself up. You will it. We all feel it comin' an' give up on the spot. We ain't that single-minded.
DON	Now just a minute...! *(Goes to argue, then sinks back)* All right, maybe I was wrong. I know what you mean. Sometimes I think it's like a conditioned reflex with me. Forcin' the pace, up against it all the time . . . Not that it's just me. We're all up against it. But don't think I wouldn't gladly sit back an' let someone else make the runnin' for once. Cos it always comes, you know. That moment. Go

Scene I

too far an' you get picked on. Singled out. Like at school. For speakin' out. Or kickin' back. *(Pause)* Only these days I'm so used to it comin', I wonder if I don't bring it on meself. Prove it's there by makin' it happen. Don't think I don't wonder. I ain't *that* single-minded.

Pause. Outside, **SANDY** *catches up with* **CAROL**

SANDY	Carol!
CAROL	What do you want?
SANDY	You can't just . . .
CAROL	What?
SANDY	Go off. We can't just let things . . . break up.
CAROL	It's not us lettin', it's him forcin'.
SANDY	He's not that bad. It's only because he cares.
CAROL	But in his own way Sandy. An' we're all supposed to follow.
SANDY	He'll apologise. I know he will.
CAROL	It's not just me. What about Jim?
SANDY	Well if his firm is involved . . .
CAROL	It's goin' a be bloody embarrassin'!
SANDY	Down the pub maybe.
CAROL	What does that mean?
SANDY	Nothing.

Pause.

CAROL	They're in it together, those two.
SANDY	In what?
CAROL	Something. They're just tryin' to make trouble.
SANDY	I thought they were tryin' to help.
CAROL	Whose side are you on anyway?
SANDY	I didn't know there were sides. I mean, you care what happens to the barn, don't you? You must've done, to get us here.
CAROL	Yeh well, maybe I was wrong. It was just . . . well, as kids we had somethin'.
SANDY	They were talkin' about another meetin'.
CAROL	Oh were they.
SANDY	Next week.
CAROL	What for?
SANDY	Organise some sort of protest . . . I don't know.
CAROL	Bastards!
SANDY	It might be fun, Carol. Bit of jumble maybe, a few games . . . You shouldn't reject it just like that.
CAROL	I don't know.

SANDY	I'd thought it'd be right up your street.
CAROL	If I come, it'll be to keep my eye on them two! *(Turns away)*
SANDY	I'll bring the key over later, shall I?
CAROL	How you gettin' home?
SANDY	Train.
CAROL	Well if you miss it, you can stay over.
SANDY	Thanks, Carol.
CAROL	'Night.

CAROL *goes.* **SANDY** *makes her way back to the barn.*

DON	I know. I blew it. I'm sorry.
DI	I just thought she'd have all the ideas, you know? Singin' round the clubs an' that. Just her sort of thing.
DON	That's right. She's got the flair. It needs a bit of razzamatazz, this thing.
GARY	That's right. After all, this place ought to mean a bit more than a clear run for a bloody carrot machine. To us, if no-one else.

SANDY *comes back in.*

DI	What did she say?
SANDY	She wasn't happy.
DON	We could see that.
SANDY	If you do meet next week, she might come. But only to keep an eye on you two.
DON	Charmin'.
DI	Least that's some progress.
SANDY	It's Jim she's thinkin' about.
DON	Aren't we all?

DI *looks at him.*

DI	All right, if it'll put people's minds at rest, I'll go an' talk to him. We need to know what he's goin' a do anyway. I'd sooner have him in than out, Don.
DON	You think I wouldn't?
SANDY	It could be embarrassin' though. With his firm bein' involved. For him an' us. That's what worries Carol.

Pause.

Will you let him know what we're plannin'?

Scene I

DON	If he lets us know what *he's* plannin'.
SANDY	Good. I'll tell Carol. When I take the key.
DI	You all right for gettin' home?
SANDY	She said I could stay if it got late.
DI	What's the civil servant goin' a say about that?
SANDY	Be a wonderful new experience for him.
DON	Becomin' a loose woman, are you?
SANDY	Oh God, what was that math teacher's name?
DI	Miss Trulock.
SANDY	You remember she discovered lipstick all over Carol's book? 'I don't know how these marks got here, but I do not approve. I do not approve of young ladies making themselves up like loose women, and I do not approve of exercise books being defaced. The owner will write a hundred times . . .'

They all laugh.

DI	Red lip marks all over it!
SANDY	That's how we got our name! The Red Mouth Gang!
GARY	Lives again!
DON	Hardly.
SANDY	Nearly though.
GARY	We could hang her in effigy.
SANDY	That's right. On a float. In the parade.

Pause.

Dress up in school uniform.

Pause.

	Be a laugh.
GARY	If you don't mind makin' a fool of yourself.
DI	What d'you mean? You'd look great in short trousers.
DON	Not if his knees are anythin' like they used to be.
DI	Are you helpin' or hinderin'?
GARY	Anyway, you'd need a lorry for a float.
DON	I can organise that. No problem.
SANDY	Decorate it up, put a piano on. Use the one from Carol's pub.
DON	Yeh well . . . We'll see.

SONG

We eat what we make from the land
What we make with the work of our hands
And that gives us strength to make more
That's what the land's for

> But while we're making
> There's others taking
> Others wasting
> What we need, we need

> Misappropriating
> Accumulating
> Then dissipating
> What we need, we need

Because they take what we make from the land
What we make with the work of our hands
Undermining our strength to make more
Money — that's not what the land's for

> But while they're cheating
> There's others meeting
> Others teaching
> What we need, we need

> Organising
> And advising
> All deciding
> What we need, we need

So we can eat what we make from the land
What we make with the work of our hands
So that gives us strength to make more
That's what the land's for!

END OF ACT ONE

* * * *

SCENE II

The barn. A week later.
DON, SANDY, GARY, DI.

DON	*(Mimicking himself as a teenager)* Right then. I hereby declare —
SANDY	Oh shut up!
DON	*(Same)* Where's Dustbin? Can't have a meetin' an' people not turnin' up!
SANDY	Way she was talkin', wild horses wouldn't keep her away.
GARY	More's the pity.
DON	*(Normal)* What about a wild super-tractor?
SANDY	I thought we needed her for the key.
DI	No, I got it off old George.
GARY	Is he comin' too?
DI	You know what he's like. 'Wouldn't want to disturb you. But I might just pop by.'
GARY	Ha!
DI	You can laugh. It's progress just to get him talkin'.
DON	Same goes for Jim. I tried to smooth things over with him. An' it's obvious he don't like bein' involved. But he will be dealing with it from now on.
DI	So what did he say?
DON	'Go ahead if you want to, but don't count on my support.'
GARY	Which means?
DON	Count on his opposition?
SANDY	That's not goin' a please Carol.
DON	I don't know what will just now. I tried talkin' to her. But she just said 'We'll see what happens at the meetin''.
SANDY	We need her help, Don.
DON	Course we do.
SANDY	I mean, I've worked out a leaflet, but we must have somewhere to leave things. The pub's ideal for that.
DI	That's right. I've photocopied some old records for a display. If we had the pub, it'd make nice pre-publicity.
DON	I've organised the lorry by the way. What about Nature Boy?
GARY	Ah.
DON	Nothin', I suppose.
GARY	One moment. *(He gets up and goes to a large parcel leant against a wall)*
DON	What's this?

DI	Don't ask me. He's been very secretive about it.

With a flourish, **GARY** *pulls back a cover to reveal the game he's made.*

SANDY	What is it?
GARY	'Spot the Farmworker'. Like at the fair. Twenty cards, all with a number on the back. An' you can't get the winnin' number 'less you stick a farmworker.
SANDY	How many of them?
GARY	One.
DI	That's not very good odds.
GARY	Realistic though. It's a chain, see. For every one farmworker there's a farmer, two blokes in the cannin' factory, a lorry driver, a wholesaler, shopkeeper, assistant an' customer.
SANDY	That's only . . . nine.
GARY	Well, these days the biggest lot is the back-up boys. One motor-worker, one chemical worker, an' the multinational managin' director who controls them an' everybody else: advertiser, market-researcher, technologist, even the bloody flavour-tester.
SANDY	Sixteen.
GARY	Well then he also controls your civil servants — one in London, one in Brussels.
SANDY	Eighteen.
GARY	Policeman an' politician.
DI	Where do they fit in?
GARY	Well you've always got them, haven't you. An' no prizes for guessin' whose pocket they're in either.
DI	Nice.
SANDY	We're all set then.
DON	Long as we can get the barn.
DI	An' that depends how far they've got with the sale. Until we know that, we don't know who to ask.
SANDY	Shame we haven't got our old tin.
DI	With the sixpences in?
SANDY	An' the hair.
DI	Where'd we put it?
SANDY	I don't know. Who had it last?
DI	Must've been Don.
GARY	It was. *(To* **DON***)* You wrote somethin', remember? Put that in too.
DON	I remember writin' somethin'. God knows where I put it though.

CAROL *comes in.*

Scene II

SANDY	Shame. Would've been nice to see the old tin again.
DI	What'd you write on it?
DON	I don't remember.
SANDY	Something violent, I bet.
CAROL	Or obscene.
DON	*(Welcoming)* Aha!
CAROL	*(Cool)* Crusaders Anonymous, is it?
DI	Just us, Carol.
CAROL	I hope this isn't going to be a waste of time. Eddie wasn't exactly delirious about me takin' the night off.
GARY	Listen, I had to come down from —
DI	*(In quick)* We were just discussin' the pub, Carol. Any chance of us usin' it?
CAROL	You're goin' ahead then?
DI	Well . . .
CAROL	Anyone talk to Jim?
DON	He's against it. An' he's goin' a be handlin' it from now on.
CAROL	That's that then. End of story.
SANDY	Not exactly, Carol.
DI	We've all been quite busy, you see.
CAROL	*(Looking at Gary's game disapprovingly)* Yes, I do.
DI	So we're keen to go ahead. With or without Jim.
CAROL	Have you got permission for the barn?
DI	Not yet, no.
CAROL	Well then! *(She laughs)*
SANDY	It doesn't have to be in here, Carol.
DI	I've talked to the Rally organisers. We can have a stall.
CAROL	I see. *(Pause)* You realise the stink this'll cause?
DON	That was the general idea, Carol.
CAROL	Yeh, but not in my pub, Don! Half Jim's office come in there lunch-time.
DI	Oh.
CAROL	They'll be off down the Sun. Eddie'll be furious.
DON	Well I'm sorry, Carol, but —
CAROL	You ain't sorry at all. This is just what you wanted.
DON	Carol, that just isn't true!
CAROL	Bloody rubbish! *(She knocks Gary's game over)*
GARY	Hey! *(Goes to its rescue)*
CAROL	You don't care what happens, do you? You don't care about people. You're against it an' that's that.
SANDY	Hark who's talkin'.
CAROL	What?
SANDY	Look what you've just done.
CAROL	You're fallin' for it too, are you?
SANDY	Fallin' for what?

CAROL	I thought we were mates, you an' me.
SANDY	We are. But you can't just... Here, Gary, let me give you a hand.
CAROL	It's crazy, the whole thing.
DI	You care about the barn, don't you?
CAROL	Yeh. But I'm also livin' in the twentieth century.

A knock at the barn door.

GEORGE	*(Outside)* You there?
CAROL	Who's that?
DI	I asked old George over. — Come in.
CAROL	You're not gettin' him involved?
DI	He was already.

GEORGE *comes in, tentative at first.*

DI	Welcome to the party, George.
CAROL	*(Aside)* In more senses'n one.
GEORGE	Well I never.
GARY	How are you, George?
GEORGE	Look at you all.
GARY	The old gang. Reunion.
GEORGE	I can see that. *(They are sitting much as they did as kids.)*
DON	You're lookin' fit, George.
GEORGE	Can't complain. I keep busy. You doin' all right?
DON	Fine.
GEORGE	Just the five of you?
SANDY	Jim couldn't come.
GEORGE	Doin' well for himself by all accounts. — Hello, Di.
DI	You heard from the Council yet?
GEORGE	No.
DI	Wanna get their fingers out.
GEORGE	They'll come up with something.
CAROL	I'm glad someone's confident.
DI	Won't do nothin' 'less you shove 'em, George.
GEORGE	I wouldn't want to hurt Mr Frankland.
DI	He's hurtin' you!
GEORGE	Not really. Been good to me over the years.
DI	He's kickin' you out!
GEORGE	Difficult times. Not his fault.
CAROL	It is if he takes it out on you, George.
GEORGE	Not him. It's these blokes from London.
GARY	What blokes?
GEORGE	I don't know. Come down in their cars of a weekend. See

Scene II

	'em round the hotel or the pub. Wearin' suits. Say they're in insurance, bankin'. Next thing you know, there's an 'en-factory or milkin'-plant goin' up.
DI	It's them that's pushin' you out, George.
GEORGE	Makin' work for people though.
GARY	Yeh, for one poor sod on his own, movin' a nozzle down a line of sixty cows' bums.
GEORGE	Can't stand in their way though. That's progress.
GARY	Don't talk daft!
CAROL	Gary!
GEORGE	Oh don't mind me. I ain't got long now anyway.
CAROL	What d'you mean?
GEORGE	I'm gettin' on, you know.

DON and **GARY** smile, shake their heads.

SANDY	You mustn't talk like that, George.
CAROL	That's right.
GEORGE	Why should I stand in their way? It's like with these Council houses. Need them for the young 'uns.
CAROL	How can you say that?
GEORGE	It's true. If they got families . . .
CAROL	Yes but . . . *(To the others)* I don't believe this. *(To* **GEORGE***)* You've got the same rights as everyone else, you know.
GEORGE	Somethin'll turn up. People always look after old folk. I know.
CAROL	The Council aren't people, George.
DON	Now now . . . some of my best friends . . . you know?
CAROL	You shut up. Sittin' there, smirkin'.
GEORGE	I'll be all right. Brought you some apples.
SANDY	*(Laughing)* Oh no!
GARY	Just like old times, eh.
SANDY	We have grown up, you know George.
GEORGE	Not to me you haven't. I got another lot in here now.
DI	What?
GEORGE	'Nother buncha kinds. Come in here just like you did.
GARY	You're jokin'.
GEORGE	Well, not exactly the same, a course.
CAROL	Listen, George, we're gettin' off the subject. You can't just sit back an' let this happen to you. Things aren't like they were in the old days. You got to stick up for yourself.

The others look at each other. **GEORGE** *bends to give* **SANDY** *the bag of apples.*

GEORGE	There are.
SANDY	Thanks, George.
CAROL	Are you listenin' to me?

GEORGE *straightens up. Pause.*

CAROL Listen, we've been talkin' . . . you know . . . about this place . . . about you an' your cottage. We thought . . . *(She looks at the others who just watch her and wait)* We thought we might help you out, you know? Bit of publicity. Draw attention to your case. A little stall maybe. In the Rally next week.

Pause.

You know, a bit of jumble, a few posters, a game or something. *(Aware of* **DON** *looking at her)* What are you starin' at?

DON	Me? I'm sayin' nothin'.
CAROL	What d'you think, George?
GEORGE	Stall, eh.
DI	Might get your pictures in the papers.
GEORGE	I like the Rally. Makes a nice change, that does.
CAROL	Good.

Pause.

DON	Thanks, Carol.
SANDY	What's Eddie goin' a say?
CAROL	Stuff Eddie. He can look after himself. Talkin' about buyin' a bloody bungalow in Yarmouth.
GEORGE	You might want your old tin then.
CAROL	What?
GARY	You haven't still got it!
GEORGE	Thinkin' about that the other day. What with these new kids. You didn't hide it very well.
DI	*(To* **DON***)* Huh!
SANDY	We were wonderin' what we'd done with it.

GEORGE *goes upstage to get tin.*

DON	Would you believe it!
DI	Fancy even botherin'.
CAROL	It's a different world.
SANDY	Now we'll find out what you wrote.

Scene II

GEORGE comes back down with tin.

GEORGE	Bit dusty, I'm afraid.
DON	*(Taking it)* Still locked.
GEORGE	I wouldn't open it.
GARY	He wouldn't either.
CAROL	Open it then. Suspense is killin' me.

DON opens the tin. They look in.

DON	Hair. Two bob in sixpences. Chewin'-gum. The old Gang Book.
DI	Where's the bit of paper?

DON takes it out. Pause.

Well?

DON *(Reads)* Woe to he who breaks the Oath
    For the Red Mouth Gang will slit his throat
    Cut it ope from ear to ear
    Shout it out for all to hear
    For this old Oath, it binds for life
    And here's the proof — the Knife!

He takes the knife out.

GARY	What we cut our thumbs with.
CAROL	Morbid little sod.
DON	Makes your blood run cold.
SANDY	Yeh well, he had an unhappy childhood.
GEORGE	Better give me that.
GARY	Too young for knives, are we George?
GEORGE	Daft you havin' it after that poem.
CAROL	Put it all back, George. Keep it safe.

GEORGE takes the tin away.

GARY	We got to do somethin' now.
SANDY	If we want to look our old selves in the eye.
DON	Long as we square it with the Union first. Don't wanna tread on their toes.
DI	Ted's all right. They're already involved. He'll go along with it.
GARY	*(Winking, to* **DI***)* Go unofficial if he don't.
DON	Not if it prejudices George's case.

CAROL	How can it? We'll keep it all dead proper. Get a few nobs along. Councillors. Always comin' in the pub. Even our MP.
SANDY	Not Joyce Knight?
CAROL	Gin an' tonic brigade.
DI	Last person to represent a rural constituency. She ever in town?
CAROL	She'll be down for the Rally.
DON	You won't get much joy out of the Housin' Committee. Sold out years ago.
SANDY	We could dig out some old photos. Then an' now.
CAROL	Food an' drink I can organise from the pub. We can make it our headquarters. Put a coupla posters up. I could even do a number.
DON	Do what?
CAROL	If no-one objects.
DON	An' there she was sayin' she'd given up.
CAROL	This is different.
DON	The old exhibitionist comin' out, eh.
CAROL	Least this time it's for a reason.

SONG

The people who know how to share
The people who know how to care
Are the people the hard ones break
The people from whom they take

> But when you're working together
> Scraping by together
> The other man's problem
> Becomes your problem too

> But when it's dog eats dog
> The ones that get eaten
> Is the one who understands
> Each other's point of view

So the people who know how to share
The people who know how to care
Will be the ones who are hard to break
The ones from whom no-one will take!

SCENE III

CAROL and SANDY, clearing the barn out.

CAROL This is what I like. Keepin' busy.
SANDY Makes a change for me, I can tell you.
CAROL Better'n bein' stuck at home, eh?
SANDY Demoralisin'. You lose your self-respect.
CAROL You don't mind the journey then?
SANDY I love it. Bounce out of bed, get 'am all fed. John's Mum comes round for the kids, an' I'm off. — What are we goin' a do with his heavy stuff?
CAROL Di an' Don'll be over lunch-time. *(Looks at her watch)* Four of us ought to shift it.
SANDY No Gary?
CAROL Too far to come when he's workin'.
SANDY I see you got old George in the papers.
CAROL Our local social column wandered in the pub, lookin' sorry for himself. Just in time for Friday's edition. He's only 22. I persuaded him this could be his big break into features. Took four lagers an' the story of his life.
SANDY An' a soggy shoulder, I suppose.
CAROL Worth it though. Now everyone comes in wantin' to know what's goin' on.
SANDY I envy you, you know.
CAROL What for?
SANDY Your energy. You never stop.
CAROL Don't dare to, do I. If I stopped to look, might not like what I saw.
SANDY I know the feelin'.
CAROL Yeh, sounded the other night like all was not roses in the dormitory suburb.
SANDY I don't know what it is. You're sort of led into it, aren't you. Handed on from mother to daughter, without question. It's only now I realise how unhappy she must have been. Mind you, didn't stop her puttin' me through it all.
CAROL Least you got some guidance. My old girl didn't even have the will to do that.
SANDY I don't love my kids, you know.

Pause. **CAROL** *stops working.*

CAROL Do what?

SANDY	I don't love my kids.
CAROL	Course you do.
SANDY	Not like mothers are supposed to.
CAROL	I don't understand.
SANDY	Nor do I. I was always told I would. It just never happened.
CAROL	You mean, there you were waitin' an' it never came?
SANDY	Sort of.
CAROL	Oh Sandy! *(She laughs)*
SANDY	Daft, en it. You go through all that discomfort, the pain an' the worry, expectin' suddenly to become a dotin' mum, an' I never did. A joke really.
CAROL	Don't sound very funny.
SANDY	*(Now she's worked up the courage)* Ain't mad about my old man either.
CAROL	Who is?
SANDY	I don't think I ever really was.
CAROL	Thought he was your Prince Charmin' when you married him.
SANDY	Shows how little I knew.
CAROL	Yeh well, can't say I'm wild about my little nest. That's what I mean about not stoppin' to think. What we need's a coupla nice fellas.
SANDY	I'm not even sure that'd do the trick.
CAROL	What d'you mean?
SANDY	I think I like women more.
CAROL	*(Slight pause)* Yeh well, no use gettin' depressed, is there. Give us a hand with this.

They work together.

CAROL	You know what? You ought to give yourself a break. Go on a spree.
SANDY	Goin' a come with me?
CAROL	Can't leave the pub, can I.
SANDY	You left it once.
CAROL	Twice'd be for good. Eddie's made that clear. Without exactly sayin' so of course.
SANDY	Least you did it once.
CAROL	Didn't get me far.
SANDY	But you do give things a go. That's what I admire.
CAROL	Used to. Gettin' too long in the tooth now.
SANDY	You're not. Look at you! Plenty of go left.
CAROL	It's really nice to hear someone say so, Sandy. Stick together, you an' me, eh. Like we used to.

Scene III

She threads her arm through **SANDY**'s. **DI** *comes in, carrying a large carton.*

DI	Aye-aye! The old axis at it again?
CAROL	What's that mean?
DI	You two. Thick as thieves. Always were. I never got a look in.
CAROL	Rubbish!
SANDY	It's true. She was always on the edge of things. We used to be really rotten to her.
CAROL	I suppose we were. I never really thought about it.
DI	It was partly my fault. I never dared join in.
CAROL	Looks like you're makin' up for it now. With a vengeance.
DI	That's right. Photocopies of every legal document relatin' to this bit of land since the year dot. Every tied cottage case in the area since the war. Statistics on the technological destruction of the soil.
CAROL	Statistics?
DI	Blind 'em with science before they starve us with it.
SANDY	Where'd you get it all?
DI	Our research department — me. I've also dug up some interestin' facts about Jim's company.
CAROL	*(Disapproving)* Oh have you.
DI	What's the word on that now?
CAROL	Don said he'd talk to him again.
DI	Well it's all there if we want it.
CAROL	Good. Start pinnin' it up then. There's the board.
DI	Don't you want to read it? Some of it might do for the pub.
CAROL	Later. When I've done this.

DI *looks at* **SANDY**, *who smiles. Suddenly, the noise of a low-flying jet.*

SANDY	God, what's that?
DI	Bloody jet. From the base down the road. Get 'em all the time round here.

They work.

SANDY	What'd you think of the other night, then?
DI	Grotesque, wasn't it.
SANDY	I enjoyed it.
DI	So did I. Except there's some memories I can do without.
CAROL	There's still one of 'em unmarried, Di.
DI	Whose benefit you announcin' that for?

CAROL	I just thought —
DI	You two spent most of the evenin' runnin' marriage down.
CAROL	Yeh well, it does have some compensations.
DI	Just don't start hearin' weddin'-bells on my account, that's all.
CAROL	You got somethin' against it then?
DI	Let's say I don't see a lot goin' for it.
CAROL	Did you ever try?
DI	Try what?
CAROL	Well, you know . . .
DI	Dollin' meself up like a birthday cake. Simperin' about?
CAROL	It don't have to take that.
SANDY	Did with us, though.
CAROL	Never!
SANDY	I should know. I used to copy you.
CAROL	We weren't that bad.
SANDY	No?
CAROL	Anyway, it wasn't me makin' the runnin' the other night.
DI	Oh?
CAROL	Don's bloody echo, you were.
DI	Never!
CAROL	*(To* **SANDY***)* That hit a nerve!
DI	Personally I always thought there was more to you an' him naggin' each other than met the eye.
CAROL	Don? I just like the way he gets things goin'. Even if they go right up my nose.
DI	What about you, Sandy? Who d'you fancy? Apart from her of course.
SANDY	Eh?
DI	You two. The inner circle.
CAROL	I've been thinkin' about that. It was only cos your Mum an' Dad never let you join in.
DI	That's right. *(Light)* I blame it all on them!
SANDY	Least you haven't gone the same way they did.
DI	I have. In lots of ways.
SANDY	Not in marriage.
DI	No, but little things, you know? Around the house. Attitudes to things. The older I get, the more I see 'em in myself.
SANDY	I know what you mean.

Short pause.

DI	So who d'you fancy?
SANDY	None of 'em really.
DI	I thought you had a thing with Gary.
SANDY	No. He had a thing with me.

Scene III

CAROL	Very romantic it was too.
DI	I always thought he liked Carol.
SANDY	Everyone liked Carol.
CAROL	Not Gary.
DI	Oh?
SANDY	Carol!
CAROL	I'm sayin' nothin'.

Pause.

DI	What a mess, eh.
SANDY	What?
DI	Sex. When you're a kid.
CAROL	You sayin' it's any better now?
SANDY	Put me off for life, I think.
DI	Never mind. You still got us. — How's that? *(Shows her work)*
CAROL	Not bad. I hope the blokes realise who the backbone of this operation is.

SONG

Get away from the dishes
Get away from the dusting
Get away from the kids
And the old man too.
There's other things you can be doing
Other ways to prove you're living
To become a human being
Just try something new.

Stand up for your rights
And an equal say
Stand up for yourself
You can get your way
Stand up for your sister
Make a start to day
Not tomorrow, not next week
But today.

Someone else can do the dishes
Someone else can do the dusting
Someone else can have the kids
And the old man too
There's other things you can be doing
Other ways to prove you're living
To become a human being
Just try something new.

Not tomorrow, not next week
But now.
Don't ask where, don't ask when
But how.

DON *comes in.*

DON	What's this then? The hen-club?
CAROL	Cheek.
DON	You may just be wastin' your time of course.
CAROL	Have you talked to Jim then?
DON	Not only is he against the idea, he's threatened to lean on the organisers to stop it.
CAROL	Oh no!
DON	His firm's got money in the Rally.
DI	Shit.
DON	Exactly.
CAROL	I hope you talked to him nicely.
DON	I was tact itself.
CAROL	I can imagine.
DON	Now listen . . . Frankland never wanted to sell in the first place. So he's on our side. An' the Rally organisers are keen cos they need the extra space. So it's goin' a take more'n Jim jumpin' up an' down to shift us.
CAROL	I hope you're right.
DI	He's always right. Didn't you know?
DON	*(Ironic)* With my experience you could always be right too.
DI	Thanks for nothin'.
SANDY	*(By the door)* So there's nothin' Jim can do?
DON	Not a thing.
SANDY	That's good, cos he's comin' up the track now. Like the Orient Express. Bloke with him can hardly keep up.
DI	*(Goes to the door)* It's Ted.
DON	What's he doin' here?
DI	It is his union.
DON	But with Jim?
DI	You did square it with him?
DON	You said he was all right.
DI	He has been so far. But I thought you were goin' to see him.
DON	I thought you — oh shit. *(Notices* **CAROL** *looking at him)* What are you grinnin' at?
CAROL	I'm just surprised the two of you didn't take minutes.
DON	That's too near the bone to be funny.
DI	*(Still brooding on it)* Damn.

Scene III

DON	All right, you two, get on that end. *(He gets a lift-hold on a heavy piece of machinery)*
DI	What for?
DON	We're goin' ahead, right? Look busy.

CAROL, DI and **DON** *take the machinery towards the door.* **JIM** *and* **TED** *enter.*

TED	Busy, Don?
DON	Oh hello.

They put the machinery down.

	Where'd you spring from?
TED	I got a call from Jim.
DON	*(To* **JIM***)* Re-joinin' the fold, are you?
JIM	Which fold's that, Don?
TED	Apparently you're havin' a bit of a protest here.
DON	I'd sooner call it a display, Ted.
TED	OK'd it with the organisers, have you?
DON	They're very keen as a matter of fact, Ted. Need the extra space, see. You know Di don't you. ASTMS. An' Carol. Sandy you don't know.
TED	Pleased to meet you.
SANDY	How d'you do.

Pause.

TED	Thing is, Don, it's this tied cottage business.
DON	Oh?
TED	Negotiations are at a very delicate stage.
DON	Sounds promisin'.
DI	What's the latest?
TED	There's a good chance George'll be rehoused.
DI	Good.
DON	By the Council?
TED	In fact, thanks to Jim.
DON	What does that mean?
TED	*(Looks at* **JIM***)* I can't reveal the details.
DI	Eh? What's goin' on?
DON	Sshh, Di.
DI	Don't you shush me.
DON	*(Ignoring this)* Why can't you reveal the details, Ted?
TED	Never mind. The point is, this stall of yours could upset things.

DON	How?
TED	I told you, negotiations are at a delicate stage.

DI joins CAROL and SANDY.

DON	Can you throw any light on this, Jim?
JIM	Ultimately it's Ted's decision.
TED	I just think it'd be better all round if you called it off.
DON	I know what you think, Ted, but you haven't told me why.
TED	You know better'n that, Don.
DON	You bet I do.
TED	I'm talkin' about confidentiality.
DON	An' I'm talkin' about withholdin' information.
CAROL	It's only a stall, Ted.
TED	An' a float, apparently.
CAROL	Well yes.
SANDY	I really think we deserve some sort of explan—
DON	We don't deserve nothin', Sandy. Not in Ted's eyes. Anythin' we want out of him, we're goin' a have to screw out. Right, Ted?
TED	The Housing Committee's involved in this too, you know.
DON	They'd have to be. — How?
TED	That's all I'm sayin'.
DI	You keepin' quiet too, Jim?
JIM	We're doin' our best for old George, that's the important part. We don't need all this.
DON	All what?
JIM	All this fuss.
DON	You mean your Company doesn't need it.

Pause. JIM says nothing.

DON	Well, unless you tell us what's goin' on, there's not a lot we can do for you.
TED	One word from us to the organisers, Don, an' there's bugger-all *you* can do.
DON	I wouldn't count on the organisers if I were you, Ted.
TED	Oh? Who we talkin' about?
DON	Now I ain't tellin'.
CAROL	*(Aside to SANDY)* Like 'High Noon', en it.
SANDY	*(Laughing, aside to CAROL)* Shut up!
TED	Listen Don, this is hardly your style. Twopenny-halfpenny protests? I don't know why you're botherin'.

Scene III

DON	If we're pushed, Ted, we don't even need the organisers. It's all been worked out. Signs up from the main road. Buntin'. We don't actually need you.
TED	Maybe not for this.
DON	What's that mean?
TED	Your union represented in the Rally?
DON	Of course.
TED	Your executive know about this?
DON	If they bother to ask, I'd say I'm here in an advisory capacity only.
TED	Bollocks.
DON	My word against yours.
TED	So what are you sayin'?
DON	You can't expect these people to stop all this, just on the strength of half-promises. Even if George was rehoused tomorrow, there's still this place.
TED	It's fallin' apart!
SANDY	We grew up here.
TED	I'm surprised to see you involved in this, Di.
DI	The feelin's mutual.
TED	Well, don't expect our co-operation in the future, that's all.
DI	Will we notice the difference?
TED	*(To* **JIM***)* Let's go.

TED and JIM go.

DON	You weren't doin' yourself a favour there, Di.
DI	I don't care. Bloody cheek!
CAROL	*(To* **DON***)* You weren't exactly diplomatic yourself.
DON	He asked for it. Comin' in here, both guns blazin'.
SANDY	*(To* **CAROL***)* High Noon was right.
DON	Jim must've said somethin' to scare him.
CAROL	Didn't scare the Red Mouth Kid though.
DON	You don't make omelettes, Carol —
CAROL	Without smashin' us down.
DON	I'm sorry. It's just that I could see what was comin'. It's no good bein' indignant in those situations. You just got to keep askin' the difficult question.
DI	You did that all right.

Pause.

DON	That's not all I did. All it needed was a word beforehand. Now this.
DI	Will he take it up with your executive?

DON   That's no problem. Trouble is, we were goin' to ask for his support on blackin' some machinery.

DI   An' you said *I* was doin' meself no favours.

Pause.

SANDY   Thanks, Don.

Pause.

CAROL   Well there's no turnin' back now. Who's goin' a help shift this heavy stuff?

    SONG

    We're making it known
    We're bringing it out into the open
    We're saying what the powers that be
    Are doing to our land.
    We've got a lot to say
    About the struggle of the people
    To lend each other
    A fighting hand.

    Shout it out, make it known
    Don't believe you're on your own
    Don't bite your tongue, sit there and stew
    There are so many just like you.

* * * * *

SCENE IV

The barn. The day of the Rally. Bunting. Flowers. Several stalls and displays. Early evening.
DI, DON and CAROL, who is by the door.

DI	Any more?
CAROL	Looks like most people have gone home.
DI	Or round the pub.
DON	Like Gary.
DI	He said he was goin' to look round the exhibits.
DON	Avoidin' the nobs, more like.
CAROL	They should've been here an' gone by now.
DI	Wouldn't mind a break myself once they've been. I've been on this all day.
CAROL	Haven't we all.
DON	What comes of bein' short-handed.
DI	I don't understand why Sandy didn't turn up.
CAROL	Somethin' must've cropped up at home. It's not as if she wasn't keen.
DI	You'd think she'd have phoned though.
CAROL	Where? We've been here all day. *(Goes back to the stall)*
DON	Maybe she an' Gary are havin' a secret tryst somewhere.
CAROL	*Not* very likely.
DON	Oh? You know somethin' I don't?
CAROL	Nothin' I'm goin' a tell you.
DON	Be like that.

Pause.

	Fancy another go? *(At Gary's dart game)*
DI	No.

Pause. She wanders to the door.

CAROL	*(With the money box)* Well we haven't done bad.
DON	For a lost cause.
DI	You think it is?
DON	We won't stop the sale. *(Throws dart)*
CAROL	Frankland might reconsider.
DON	He can't afford to. *(Throws second dart)* With the best will in the world.
DI	At least he delayed.

DON	Only out of decency. *(Throws last dart)* An' as long as we were makin' a fuss.
DI	You sayin' we won't be in the future?
DON	Can *you* twist their arm?

Pause.

CAROL	I was just surprised we didn't hear from Jim again.
DON	Yeh. Disappointin' that. He might at least have put up a fight.
DI	Specially after all the trouble we went to. Can't say we weren't ready for him.
DON	I'd love to know what deal he was offerin' the Council.
DI	*(By the door)* Now's your chance to find out.
CAROL	They comin'?
DI	Les from the Housin' Committee. Joyce Knight. An' — oh no.
DON	Who?
DI	Our friend Ted.
DON	That's all right. He thinks the sun shines out MP's backsides. If he gets nasty, we'll set Joyce on him.
CAROL	You'll do no such thing. *(She takes out bottles of gin and tonic and a small tray of snacks)*
DON	What's all this?
CAROL	Might as well get things off to a good start.
DON	An' we been standin' here parched for the last two hours!
CAROL	Knowin' you, you'd have finished it off single-handed.
DON	You're so corruptible, Carol.
CAROL	Me? I'm doin' the corruptin'.
DI	How we goin' a handle this? You goin' a mention that deal?
DON	See what they say first.

LES *at the door. Behind him,* **JOYCE** *and* **TED**.

LES	Can we come in?
DON	It is your borough, Les.
LES	*(Jokey)* The electors might have something to say about that.
DON	They probably will, next time around.
LES	You know Joyce, don't you. And Ted.
DON	This is Di. ASTMS.
DI	*(Mainly of* **TED***)* Well, this *is* an honour.
JOYCE	Not at all. We're all in favour of this sort of thing, aren't we Ted.
TED	In principle, why not?

Scene IV

DI	And in practice?
JOYCE	*(Confidential)* We prevailed upon him. — I must say you've done a lovely job.
DON	Four weeks hard labour. An' felt like it sometimes.
JOYCE	But all in a good cause. — Don't you think?
LES	Very nice.
TED	Not bad at all.
DI	This is a change of heart then, Ted?
TED	More of circumstances, Di.
DI	Oh?
CAROL	Well, whatever the reason, we're really glad you could come, aren't we. — Have you see this, Joyce? The historical side. That's Di's contribution.
JOYCE	*(Looks at it)* Fascinating. And a lot of hard work, I imagine. What a shame it's only for a day.
DI	Actually, it's been up in the pub all week.
JOYCE	Ah.
CAROL	*(In quick)* That reminds me. I thought you might like a drink, Joyce. After your trek out all this way.
JOYCE	Well I must admit, walking round all afternoon . . .
CAROL	Les? Ted?
TED	You haven't got a beer?
CAROL	Sorry.
DON	For you, Ted, anything. *(He fetches some cans from a bag)*
CAROL	An' you were makin' remarks at me!
DON	Emergency ration.

They all get drinks.

	Question is, Ted, is there anything to celebrate?
TED	How d'you mean?
DON	This 'change of circumstances'. Have you found George a house yet?
TED	Don't look at me.
LES	There's been a hitch, Don.
DON	Oh?
LES	There's no threat to George, mind. But it's no longer certain the purchase will go through.
DI	You mean, Jim's firm isn't buyin'?
LES	Frankland isn't selling.
DI	Why not?
LES	No idea. He suddenly got cold feet. Pulled out.
DI	Not because of us?
LES	He wouldn't say.
DON	What then?

LES	*(Shrugs)* Ask *him*.
DI	*(To* **TED***)* Is this why you've left us alone?
TED	That's right.
DON	What did Frankland say exactly?
LES	Only that he wouldn't give his reasons now. But they'd become apparent in due course.
DI	Very mysterious.
DON	The whole thing is. *(To* **LES***)* Like your deal with Jim's firm.
LES	What deal?
DON	They must've offered you something.
LES	Don't know what you're talking about.
DON	Oh come on, you can do better'n that.
CAROL	*(In quick)* Have you seen our game, Joyce?
DON	Carol —
CAROL	'Spot the Farmworker'.
JOYCE	Oh, this looks interesting.
DI	10p a go.
CAROL	Oh I think for Joyce —
JOYCE	No I insist. Come on, Les.

LES *pays.* **CAROL** *gives* **JOYCE** *darts.*

	Who are all these little men?
DI	They're the middlemen involved in agriculture.
JOYCE	How clever.
DON	Actually it's monoculture.
JOYCE	*(About to throw)* I'm sorry?
DON	Why the barn's comin' down. *(Partly to* **TED** *and* **LES***)* In this 'corporate' age, to be more competitive, the drive is towards one huge farm producin' one huge capital-intensive crop. An' one tiny little bloke doin' it. Right, Ted? To win, you have to hit him with the hardware.
JOYCE	He is tiny too.
DI	*(Pointing to the cards)* But he still needs more muscle than a lorry driver, more skill than a motor mechanic an' more naus than a soil expert.
TED	*(Beginning to enjoy himself)* But not more wages, eh.

JOYCE *throws.*

DI	Though we pay higher prices — thanks to all the processin' an' modern marketin'.
TED	An' the EEC. Eh, Joyce?

JOYCE *throws.* **JIM** *comes in, unseen.*

Scene IV

CAROL	I don't think Joyce wants to —
DON	So while Labour goes on supportin' it an' the big companies get richer, you, me an' the soil get poorer.

JOYCE throws.

JOYCE	Have I won?
DI	No-one does, Joyce.
CAROL	Would you like one of these?

JOYCE gives LES the darts and takes a snack from CAROL.

DI	The only time anyone wins is when it's left idle as an investment. Or used for rent. An' then it's the landowner who benefits.
JIM	Not necessarily.
CAROL	Jim!
DON	What are you doin' here?
JIM	Lookin' for him. *(Les)*
LES	Oh?
JIM	Haven't you told them yet?
LES	Told them what?
JIM	About Frankland.
LES	Not selling, you mean?
JIM	He's sellin' all right. To the Ministry of Defence.

Short pause.

DI	What for?
JIM	I've been chasin' these two all day to find out.
LES	I'm sorry. This is the first I've heard about it.
TED	Me too.
JIM	So you've no idea what's behind it?
LES	None at all.
JIM	Who does then? Months my firm's been in negotiation, and they waltz in... *(To JOYCE)* They can do this, I suppose?
JOYCE	Seems they already have.
JIM	Well I want to know why! The whole thing's been shrouded in secrecy. They've gone straight over everyone's heads. Made a mockery of all this... *(the display, etc.)*
JOYCE	Well we certainly ought to find out.
JIM	Damn right we should.
DON	I wouldn't count on it.
JIM	What d'you mean?

DON	Well if it's the Ministry of Defence... Why d'you think you haven't heard anything so far?

Pause.

JOYCE	Don has a point of course.
DI	Yeh but surely we've a right to know —
LES	Actually no. We haven't.
DI	I beg your pardon!
LES	Official Secrets.
JIM	We're not in a police state yet, are we?

Pause.

JOYCE	Well quite. But I do think we need to find out first exactly what is planned.
DI	And when you do, Joyce, we'd be glad to hear about it.
JOYCE	We'll certainly keep you informed. Of course.
DI	I mean more than that. Come down an' talk to us. Explain what's goin' on. An' why.
JOYCE	Well if time permits —
TED	I think we're entitled to some sort of explanation, Joyce.
JOYCE	Of course. But Don's right. This isn't an easy area.
DI	We're not goin' to give up, you know, Joyce. Just because the Government's involved. For us it's still the same issue.
JOYCE	I appreciate that, Di, but —
DI	If we're kept in the dark, that's all the more reason to carry on.
JOYCE	I assure you —
DI	We've a right to know!

Pause.

JOYCE	I think Les and I need to talk this over.
LES	It's not directly my —
JOYCE	No Les, but as local man...
TED	We are your constituents, Joyce.
JOYCE	I'm aware of that, Ted. *(To* **LES***)* Perhaps we should be getting along.
LES	Oh right. Ready when you are, Joyce.
JOYCE	Thank-you so much, Carol. It really was interesting. Such good work. And the drink was very welcome.
CAROL	My pleasure.
JOYCE	*(To the others)* I will do what I can.

LES *and* **JOYCE** *go.* **TED** *hesitates.*

Scene IV

JIM	You goin' or stayin', Ted?
TED	Tell you the truth, I'm not sure.
JIM	I thought you Labour mafiosi stuck together.
TED	Not on this kind of thing.
DI	Changed your tune, Ted?
TED	It's not me that's changed.
DON	They might know more'n they're lettin' on of course.
TED	I don't think so. Not this time.
CAROL	Not for want of you givin' 'em the opportunity either.
DON	There's more'n one cover-up goin' on here, Carol.
JIM	*(To TED)* Maybe you ought to stick with 'em? Least you might find out what there is to know.
TED	Playin' informer now, am I?
JIM	Why not? It's either that or the blind leadin' the blind.
TED	Why me, though?
JIM	Who else is there?
TED	*(Decides)* I'll see you.

TED *goes hurriedly.*

DI	*(To JIM)* Well, welcome back! Nothing like knowing who your real friends are.
DON	He's just worried someone's goin' a change their mind again.
JIM	I'm fed up with bein' messed around, Don. Ted knows what's what.
DON	Nothin' like a foot in both camps, is there.
DI	'Ark who's talkin!
JIM	That's right. You'd do the same.
CAROL	He already was. One minute goin' for Les's jugular, the next quotin' the Official Secrets Act.
DON	*(To JIM)* Exactly what deal were you offerin' Les anyway?
CAROL	I've had enough of this. What right've you got —
DON	What right've *they* got!
CAROL	You just blunder in, ridin' roughshod over everyone . . .
DI	Not everyone, Carol.
CAROL	That's right, you defend him.
DI	I will.
CAROL	An' I know why.
DI	Oh really, Carol!
CAROL	Good as drove her out, you did.
JIM	Now come on —
CAROL	An' you're no better.
JIM	Wha—?
CAROL	First you try an' stop us, then we don't see hide nor hair of

DON	you for two weeks, then you turn up at the last minute an' destroy everything! Just when we were gettin' somewhere! Fat chance with those two.
CAROL	Only cos they wouldn't trust you to post a letter. An' I don't blame 'em. *(To* **JIM**) An' as for you —
JIM	Listen, Carol, if you think I'm goin' a let myself be pushed around by the Labour in-crowd —
CAROL	Oh!
DON	Now just a minute —

GARY *walks in.*

GARY	Oh, havin' a party, are we?
DON	Where the hell've you been?
GARY	I told you. Lookin' around. Seein' what mechanical monsters they got in store for us next year.
DI	Skyvin' off, more like.
GARY	Yeh well, people like that get up my nose.
CAROL	That's only the half of it. If Sandy'd been here, it would've been a different story.
GARY	What's that supposed to mean?
DI	Carol, we don't need —
CAROL	*(Close to tears)* I went to a lot of trouble over this.
DI	We all did, Carol.
GARY	*(To others)* What's goin' on?
DI	Jim's firm isn't buyin' the land any more. The Ministry of Defence is.

Pause.

GARY	Another bloody base, I suppose.

Pause. **DI** *realises he's right.*

DI	Of course.
DON	Trust Nature Boy to get it first time.
GARY	So what's happenin' to old George?
JIM	He'll be all right. If it's a Government purchase, they'll have to re-house him.
GARY	So we're back where we started.
DI	'Cept now it's the Government we got to keep an eye on.
CAROL	Don't you ever stop?
DI	Do they? This is the second time we've been caught nappin'.
DON	The third if you count the Oath.

Scene IV

DI	Whatever we plan, they're always one jump ahead.
GARY	*(To* **JIM***)* I suppose they can do this?
JIM	They already have. Took us weeks of bloody shoppin' around, they waltz in an' claim it just like that.
DON	Least it's nice to know someone in this day an' age can stymie a multinational.
JIM	You're not startin' that now?
DON	Why not? If you believe in the State, it's important to defend it.
JIM	I hope you're jokin'.
DON	Not entirely, no.
DI	I thought you went a bit quiet when that came up.
JIM	It's a joke. We couldn't defend ourselves in the World Cup, let alone a war.
DON	More'n one reason for an army. Protects your trade, your foreign interests. I'd have thought you'd be all for that.
JIM	Free trade yeh, but not tanks in the streets!
DON	You believe in a myth then. Wherever this country's had free trade, the army's been not far behind.
JIM	Don't tell me after all your bellyachin' about us, you're still backin' the Empire!

SANDY *comes in, unseen.*

DON	Not the Empire, the State. No good bein' squeamish about power. You wouldn't have backed off our little protest here if we hadn't shown a bit of resistance.
JIM	It wasn't you that did it, it was the bloody Government!
DON	That's right. The State. It's an ill wind, you know . . .
JIM	If you're goin' a protest about anything, it ought to be about them interferin'.
DI	That mean you're comin' over to our side, Jim?
JIM	Depends if you're carryin' on.
DI	I don't know. Are we? We haven't talked about it.
DON	I'm not sure we are.
DI	Oh?
DON	Well what chance do we stand?
DI	We could still make our voice felt.
SANDY	While we've still got a voice left.
CAROL	Sandy! Where've you been?
SANDY	Havin' a fat, flamin' row with my so-called husband, that's where.
CAROL	What about?
SANDY	This place.
CAROL	Why?
SANDY	Ever since he's known about it he's been actin' strange.

55

	Hasn't said nothin' of course. So last night I had a look in his briefcase. This place is on the acquisition programme connected with cruise missiles.
DI	Oh no.
GARY	That's all we need.

Pause.

CAROL	*(Picking up the gin)* Anyone else?
GARY	Let's go round the pub, Carol. Least we can get off our feet there.
DON	An' drink what we like.
SANDY	Why leave though? We ought to be lockin' ourselves in. Ready for the bulldozers.

Pause.

DI	You'd do that?
SANDY	Well that's what it comes down to, isn't it? I've had a whole train journey to think about it. What else can we do?
GARY	We need to think it over too, Sandy.
DI	It's too much for one day.
GARY	*(Quiet)* Come on.

They go. **CAROL** *and* **JIM** *hang behind.*

CAROL	I'll lock up.

While **CAROL** *clears up and gets her things,* **JIM** *talks.*

JIM	See Carol, I know what Don means about the big companies throwin' their weight about. But it's not only us do it. We can see that now. At least when we do it we're helpin' to produce somethin', get somethin' goin'. What I can't stand is people sittin' around belly-achin', bein' negative. Politics. In the end it's destructive. When do they ever *do* anything?
CAROL	They do what they can, Jim. It's not as if they don't care.
JIM	I care!
CAROL	Anyway, where would they get without you? *(Pause. She's ready)* We're goin' a need you, Jim.
JIM	God knows what they'll say at work.
CAROL	Come on. We don't want the others talkin'.

They go.

SONG

> Reunion
> We're back together here
> The Union
> Lends us a willing ear
> The Union
> Speaks for all working men
> Reunion
> We are all one again

A hundred years ago some had to starve
While 'Men of Progress', bled the soil
To make their own part of the country rich
But not the part of those who gave their toil

> Reunion
> We're back together here
> The Union
> Lends us a willing ear
> The Union
> Speaks for all working men
> Reunion
> We are all one again

But now because the tide of history's turning
Men of progress look a different way
The voice is heard of those who shared starvation
In those who work to share the land today

> Reunion
> We're back together here
> The Union
> Lends us a willing ear
> The Union
> Speaks for all working men
> Reunion
> We are all one again

END OF ACT TWO

* * * * *

SCENE V

The barn. Evening, a week later. Chairs are set out informally.
CAROL, SANDY, DON, GARY, JIM and TED, who has just arrived.

TED	You don't mind?
CAROL	More the merrier.
TED	I mean, I know we crossed swords before —
CAROL	Have a seat.
TED	You got any minutes I could look at?
CAROL	Sorry?
TED	You know — aims, principles, a constitution.

CAROL *turns to* **SANDY**.

SANDY	This is our first proper meetin'.
GARY	We never bothered before.
DON	Maybe it's time we started.
GARY	Oh?
DON	If we're askin' people to join us, they ought to know what they're gettin' into.
GARY	We don't even know ourselves yet.
DON	All the more reason. — Especially if we're gettin' the Press along.
GARY	Yeh but we don't want to get bogged down in bureaucracy before we even start.
TED	Knowin' where you stand ain't bureaucracy.
JIM	Ted's right. This isn't just a few friends any more. Ultimately we're up against the Government, the military, even NATO. We've got to be organised.
GARY	Who by? You?
JIM	I didn't mean —
DON	Who's chairin' this?
GARY	See what I mean?

DI *comes in.*

DI	Sorry I'm late. — She isn't here yet then?
GARY	Probably turn up after we've finished — in a private jet.
JIM	We need someone to chair, Di. An' someone to put the other case.

Scene V

CAROL	What d'you mean 'the other case'?
JIM	Well she is on record as bein' against unilateral disarmament.
CAROL	Oh no.
JIM	Didn't you know?
GARY	I'll do it.

Looking around, they turn to DI.

DI	All right, I'll chair.
SANDY	Maybe if I took minutes, I could draft some sort of constitution?

No-one disagrees.

CAROL	We'd better sort these chairs out.

They do.

JIM	*(To CAROL)* I thought it was you invited her?
CAROL	No. I reminded her a couple of times. After the Rally. But Don fixed the date.

The chairs are set.

GARY	Is this the shape of things to come then?
DI	What d'you mean?
GARY	If we've got to have a constitution, it ought to spell out we're non-political.
DON	Nothin's non-political.
GARY	All right, non-*party* political. We don't want to become just another arm of the Labour movement.
DON	What's so terrible about that?
GARY	This is a bigger issue, that's all.
TED	It has its advantages, Gary.
GARY	Like what?
TED	A lot of support for a start. One resolution through a branch is worth a hundred signatures in the street.
DON	It's muscle, Gary. You heard Jim say what we're up against. We need a bit of our own.
GARY	Do we? How d'you think we got in this situation? There's goin' a be 160 cruise missiles, all over East Anglia. An' never mind all the cock about defence and deterrents, these are *attackin'* weapons. Muscle. Designed to get in first. So what does that make us? Number One Target. That's where 'muscle' gets you.

TED But if you could organise the air force, you might stop 'em bein' used.
DON An' if you organised the workers who made 'em, you could even stop 'em existin'.
JIM But that isn't goin' to happen, Don. An' meanwhile it's *everyone* who's affected by this. Families, women an' children. They haven't got 'muscle'.
CAROL That's right. It's a moral issue.
DON So what d'you suggest? Prayin'?
GARY We can only start with what we've got.
DON An' Ted's offerin' you his branch. What's wrong with that?
GARY What price does it come at?
TED I don't understand.
CAROL I do. We'll get tarred with their brush. Right? They may support us, but do we support them?
TED I'm not askin' you to.
CAROL But it doesn't stop there, does it. In return for your 'muscle', you finish up tellin' us what to think.
DI But Carol, the Left has always been against nuclear weapons.
GARY I suppose that's why the arms race is with the Communist bloc.
DON Only because they've had to defend 'emselves.
GARY Have they?
DON Would you trust the Pentagon? ITT? Krupp?

GARY doesn't answer.

DI The Russians haven't even got the upper hand, Gary. Maybe in conventional weapons, but not in nukes. It's the Yanks who won't sign SALT 2, don't forget.

Pause.

Anyway, I don't see why you're bein' so defensive. You vote Labour, you're in the union.
GARY It's bad enough bein' involved in this, let alone —
DI What?
GARY Well, the people in my village. I've been tellin' 'em all about the barn, you know, an' they've been really sympathetic. Get 'em on this though, they treat you like a leper.
CAROL I've had the same in the pub.
DON What d'you expect? If you wanna make yourself unpopular, believe in somethin' that's not goin' a make people rich. I get that all the time.
GARY Yeh but you are a ravin' Red. I ain't.

Scene V

DI	These things do affect people, Don. You can't ignore 'em.
DON	Don't mean you let 'em make your mind up though.
JIM	No, but I've had to keep quiet about this at work. An' word still gets around. Especially if it's not what people expect.
DON	Ruined next year's promotion, have you?
JIM	It's no laughin' matter, Don.
DI	Well if we're talkin' about sacrifices . . . *(She looks at* **SANDY***)*
GARY	What?
DI	I'm sorry. Maybe I shouldn't have mentioned it.

Pause.

SANDY	John's stayin' with a friend in London. That's all.

Pause. **SANDY** *goes back to her notes.*

DI	Well I don't know how we put all that in a constitution.
JIM	The point is, we'll be seen as political whatever we say.
DON	So we might as well know what we want.

JOYCE *and* **LES** *come in, unnoticed at first.*

	Is it just cruise missiles we're against? All nuclear weapons? The whole arms race? Nuclear power?
GARY	Yes.
DON	What d'you mean, 'yes'?
GARY	The lot.
DON	Well I'm sorry, I don't like the idea of cruise missiles on British soil, but I'm not against anythin' an' everythin' nuclear.
DI	*(Who's seen* **JOYCE***)* Don.
DON	What? *(Sees* **JOYCE***)* Oh.
JOYCE	Sorry I'm late. Have you started already?
DI	Only just, Joyce. Have a seat.
JOYCE	Do we have one for Les?
LES	I'll be all right here, thanks. *(He sits with the 'body' of the meeting)*
JOYCE	Well don't let me stop the flow. How are we doing this? As a talk, a debate, or just an informal thing?
DI	Well . . .
GARY	Debate.
DON	We haven't even got a motion yet. *(To* **GARY***)* I mean, what are you sayin'? Are you against all defence spendin' too?

GARY	Yeh. Sort of.
DON	What sort of answer's that!
GARY	Well, what are *you* proposin' anyway?
DON	I'm just sayin' be specific. At the moment we don't even know for sure what the land's bein' bought for.
GARY	We don't know anythin'. That's the trouble.
DI	Maybe Joyce could help us out on that.
JOYCE	Well of course it's terribly difficult to get a straight answer on these things, but it does appear the Ministry is involved in several purchases connected with the re-think on Defence.
GARY	We knew that already. What's the point of pussy-footin' around in Westminster? It's down here it's happenin', an' it's down here we ought to be fightin' 'em!
DON	All right, but if we're gettin' into a fight, we ought to know what we're fightin' for.
CAROL	Who says it's a fight?
GARY	Well it is. An' if we're goin' a be hung for bein' political, it might as well be for a sheep as a lamb.
DON	I'm sorry, the issues around nuclear energy an' the arms race are very different.
GARY	Not in the end. It's all the same bloody fiddle.
DON	Maybe it is. But you can't invoke the whole bloody spectrum, then blame people for bein' political. Either we concentrate on one issue we can win, or we'll lose. Like last time.
DI	Maybe Joyce —
JOYCE	I'd like to know what other people think.

Pause.

JIM	Well I agree with Don. I'm against the arms race, but I don't think you can put the clock back. Nuclear power is here. An' if you take the energy crisis seriously, we ought to harness it.
GARY	But they haven't! They can't control it! They don't even know what to do with the waste!
DI	Gary.
GARY	Sorry.
JIM	Obviously everything should be done to make it safe.
GARY	The wind an' the sea have been safe for years.
DON	Hurricanes? Storms?
JIM	Listen, I'm all in favour of alternative energy, but the technology isn't there to develop it yet. The technology for nuclear energy is.
GARY	Only cos it'll make someone a fat profit.

Scene V

JIM	But it is there.
GARY	An' it could blow up any minute.
DON	You could get knocked down, crossin' the road.
DI	Ted?
TED	I agree with Jim on that. But I was in CND in the sixties an' I don't like nuclear weapons. What I wonder though is how a call for unilateral disarmament can work now, on its own. No-one's goin' a give up what they've already got. But we should be able to stop escalation.
DI	Carol?
CAROL	It's the fightin' I'm against. The bullyin'. Men's toys.
JOYCE	But if Russia invaded tomorrow, you'd want to be defended, wouldn't you?
CAROL	Not that way.
DON	But you'd expect some bloke to turn out an' do his bit for you.
CAROL	I don't know if I would. Look at the last two wars. Women sendin' their blokes off . . . for what?
DON	To fight bloody fascism, that's what.
CAROL	But it's always men. Generals an' — excuse me, Joyce — politicians tellin' people to fight. I can see why *they* want it. But why should *I*?
DON	Sooner red than dead, Carol?
CAROL	Least while there's life there's hope. I mean, look at Poland.
GARY	That's right. The Poles have resisted spendin' more on defence. So have the Rumanians.
CAROL	You see? Maybe if people over there and over here sort of linked up . . . I don't know.
GARY	The Dutch've postponed their decision on Cruise. The Italians made it conditional on America signin' SALT 2. The Belgians an' West Germans wants talks on disarmament. It's only us who've agreed. Unconditionally! — I wanna know what Joyce thinks about *that*.
JOYCE	Well I certainly think the decision was rash. And I'm very well aware that it endangers the whole of Europe.
GARY	Endangers! The super-powers are usin' us as their bloody battlefield!
DON	But why is it, Gary, that no-one's just turned round an' stuck two fingers up at the Yanks?
JIM	Don has a point. We are part of NATO, don't forget. Our defence systems are inter-connected. There are economic benefits —
GARY	An' a hundred bloody US military establishments up an' down the country!
JOYCE	But surely you're not saying we shouldn't have defence of any kind at all?

Pause. **GARY** *can't answer.*

	And having said that, surely it's important we have the best, and that it costs us as little as possible.
LES	If they want it, let them pay for it.
TED	But the price we pay is that we can't choose the company we keep. Their enemies become our enemies.
LES	But it's precisely because of that, because there have been two major alliances lined up ready to obliterate each other for thirty years, that the peace has been kept!
SANDY	An' to end it, it just takes one lunatic — on either side.
JIM	Or a terrorist, stealin' plutonium.
DON	But how d'you stop *him*, Jim? *Force.*
CAROL	That doesn't mean it's right. I mean, what if everyone in Europe just said 'No'?
JOYCE	Well let me say here and now that I'm well aware of these dangers and I'm all in favour of the pressure for multilateral disarmament being kept up.
TED	But Joyce, we've been talkin' multilateral disarmament for years. Where's it got us?
JOYCE	The difficulty, Ted, lies in persuading the other side to join you.
DON	That's right. Gettin' rid of our bombs doesn't mean gettin' rid of theirs. People don't give up power just like that. You should know that, Ted. You've got to horse-trade.
TED	I can understand that, Don. What I don't understand is why you're takin' this line. Carol's got a point. If the whole of Europe turned round tomorrow an' said 'No', who could stop us?
DON	If you turn the other cheek, you'll get it slapped. If you wanna stop a war, you negotiate.
LES	And preferably from a position of strength.
GARY	What strength? All we've got is our lives.
TED	That's right. We're talkin' about what *we* want, not what our leaders want. You also go in askin' for more than you expect to get, don't forget.
DON	But we haven't even gone in yet. We don't know what we want. Even in here there are half a dozen different points of view.
CAROL	An' it's not as if it's easy to get people involved in this. The ones I've talked to in the pub just seem to accept it. The biggest-ever threat to their lives an' they just shrug. They don't believe they can do anythin'.
JIM	'Cept dig a hole an' build a shelter.
DI	If you're one of the few hundred can afford ten grand to do it.

Scene V

GARY Then *they* push the button an' the rest of us fry.
JIM An' the more people think like that, about minimisin' the destruction, the more chance it'll happen. Subconsciously people are preparin' for it.

Pause.

TED A mass outcry now against nuclear weapons —
LES Won't succeed like one against Cruise alone.
TED But that's goin' back on party policy. This was decided at Conference.
LES But how can it be implemented?
TED By doin' it. Same as the re-selection of MP's.
LES Aren't we straying off the subject here?
TED I don't know. Are we? Are you still standin' for your National Executive, Don?
DON What's that got to do with it?
TED I just wondered. Knowin' your union's line on this.
LES I don't see what this has to do with —
TED The other thing about negotiation is the first thing the bosses ask when you go in: Can you *deliver*?
DON I believe what I believe, Ted. Not what's expedient.
TED Just as well you believe what you do though, isn't it?
JOYCE Perhaps Les is right. We do seem to be getting off the point.
DON Nothin' I've said precludes a campaign for multilateral disarmament. It's a question of how you spearhead it, that's all.

Pause.

DI You haven't said much, Sandy.
SANDY I've been takin' notes.
CAROL But what do you think?
SANDY I'm against the lot. An' nothin' I've heard changes that. I don't care what we call our campaign. I said I'd lie down in front of the bulldozers, an' I meant it.

SONG

It's there
We're here
It should be ours
We should work it together
It's there
We're here
We should be one
It should belong to us

Landmark

> The land isn't there
> To be divided
> Except between us
> For the good of all
> And we're not here
> To be divided
> We stand together
> For the good of all
>
> It's there
> We're here
> It should feed us
> We should work it together
> It's there
> We're here
> Let's make it work
> Let's make it work for us!

SCENE VI

The barn. Darkness. Before dawn.
A TELEVISION DIRECTOR and TECHNICIAN surrounded by their equipment.

DIRECTOR What's happened?
TECH. Fuckin' lamp's packed up.
DIRECTOR Aren't there any lights?
TECH. Somewhere.
DIRECTOR I want all this lot set up by first light.
TECH. I don't need tellin' six times, you know.

Slight pause.

DIRECTOR What's that?
TECH. What?
DIRECTOR Outside.

CAROL, SANDY, DI and **GARY** *outside.*

DI Got the key?
CAROL It's open.
DI What?
CAROL Look.

The door opens. Blue light. They come in.

GARY Funny.
CAROL There's someone in here.
DIRECTOR Only us.
GARY Who?

CAROL *puts the lights on.* **TV DIRECTOR** *and* **TECHNICIAN** *are revealed.*

GARY What's all this?
SANDY It's the telly.
GARY How'd you get in here?
DIRECTOR Same way you did. Are you the demonstrators?
CAROL What?
DIRECTOR We heard there was going to be a protest.
CAROL Where'd you hear that?

DIRECTOR	Around. We finished our last job early, so we thought we'd hang on. — Are you?
CAROL	We just saw them puttin' the fence up yesterday.
DIRECTOR	So did we.
GARY	Didn't do 'em much good did it.
DIRECTOR	Perhaps if they'd finished it . . .
GARY	That an' just one nightwatchman.
DIRECTOR	Thank God for the cuts, eh!

Pause.

DI	Are you official?
DIRECTOR	Good vantage point, you see. If anything happened, we'd scoop the other side.
GARY	You didn't answer her question.
DIRECTOR	We could *become* official.
SANDY	Fame at last, Carol. You goin' a sing?
GARY	So what were you expectin'? Placards? Molotov cocktails?
DIRECTOR	Just waiting to see what happened.
DI	Whose side are you on in this?
DIRECTOR	We're supposed to be neutral.
DI	What does that mean?
DIRECTOR	What it says.

Pause.

On the other hand, we wouldn't be here if we hadn't made the effort.

Pause.

SANDY   Where d'you want us?

SONG

> They tell us growth's a good thing
> On that they all agree
> But what they grow is for themselves
> And not for you and me
>
> Growing, growing, growing, gone
> You and me and everyone
> Growing, growing, growing, gone
> Our lives are over before they're begun
>
> Growth can be a good thing
> On that we can agree
> But not until the land we work
> Belongs to you and me.

END

THE SONGS

Each song required a different approach musically: I aimed at creating an underlying impression of disparity and variety. The music was composed to suit practical requirements of mood in the text and lyrics, but unresolved in the final analysis as the attitudes and political stances of the characters themselves. The ambiguity and unresolved quality is portrayed by the predominant jazz-based dissonance and use of minors. The bold majors — like primary colours in music — are used less, and reflect solidarity as in 'The Hoop'.

NICOLLE FRENI

GROWING

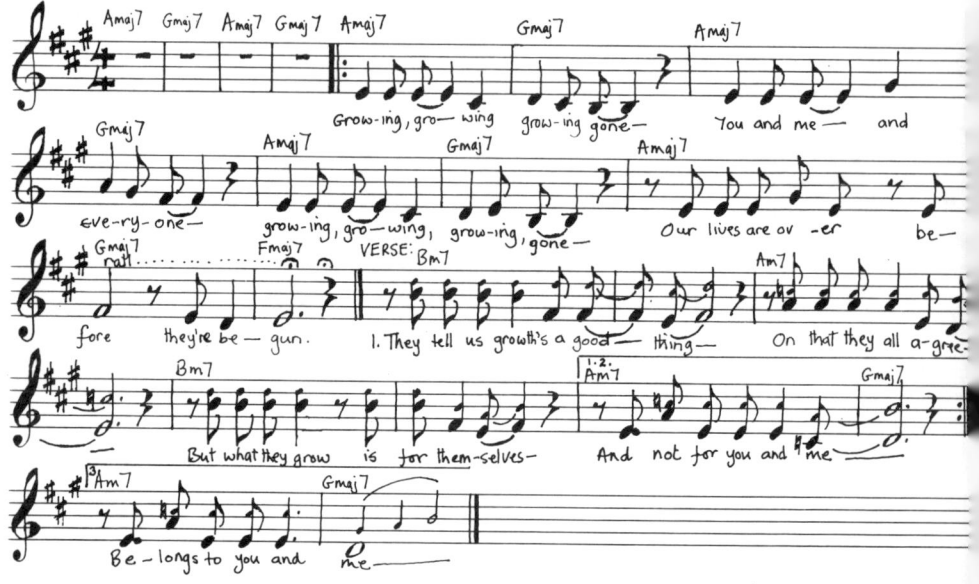

WE'VE BEEN THROUGH THE HOOP

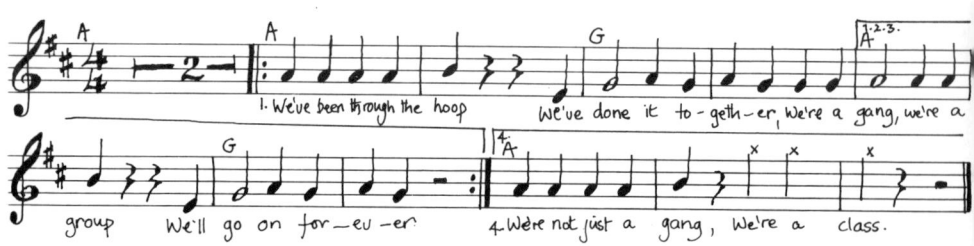

GETTING OLDER

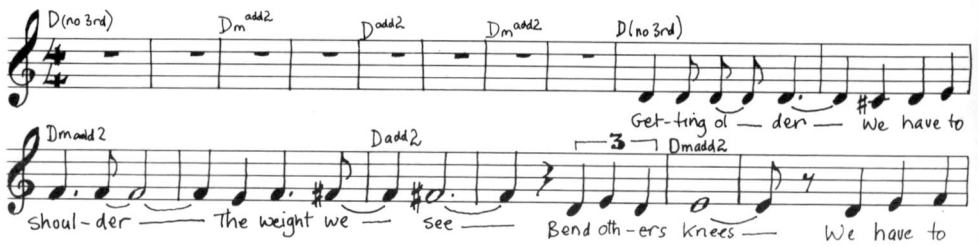

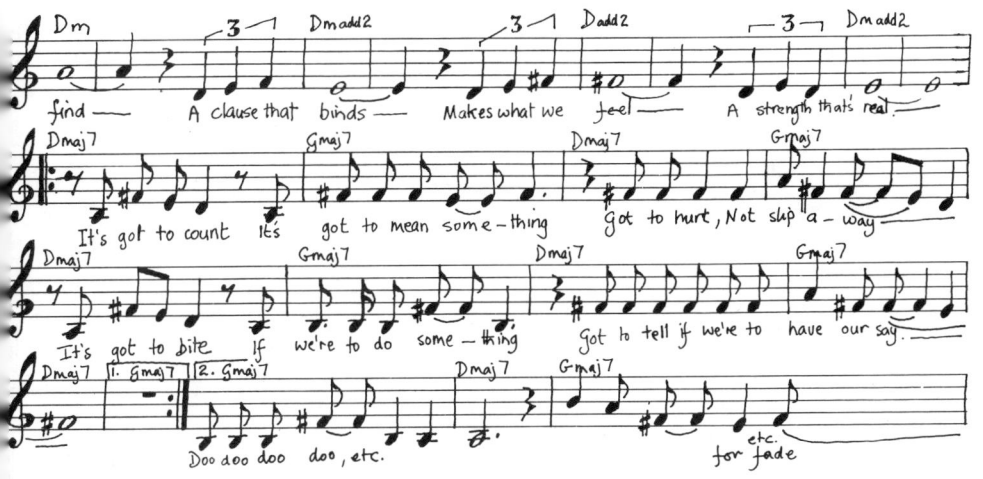

WE EAT WHAT WE MAKE

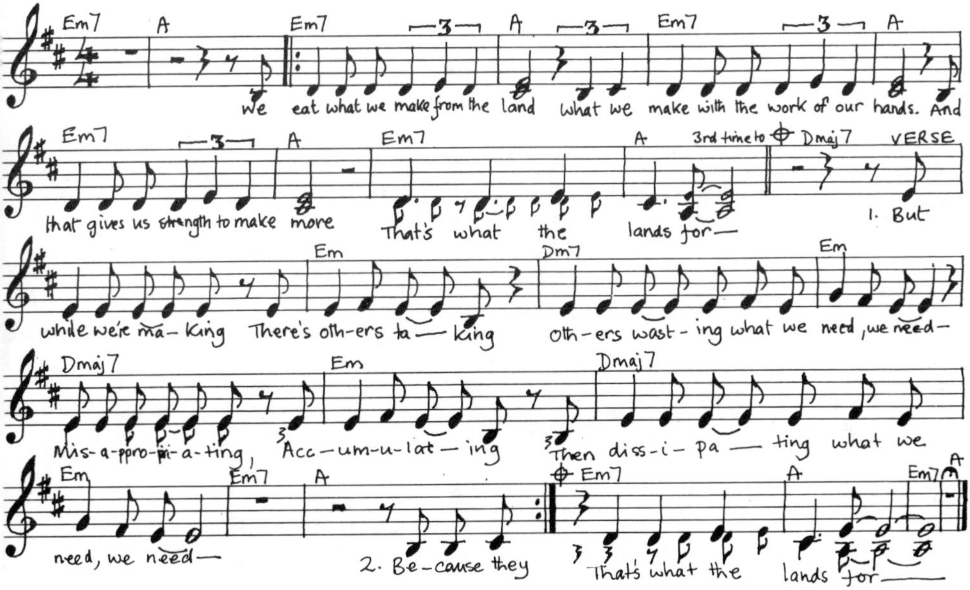

THE PEOPLE WHO KNOW

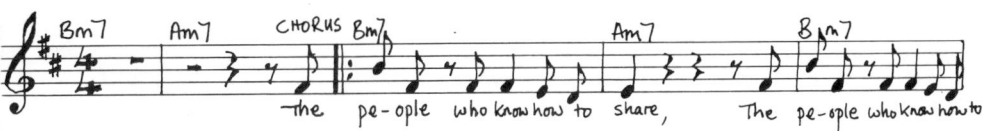

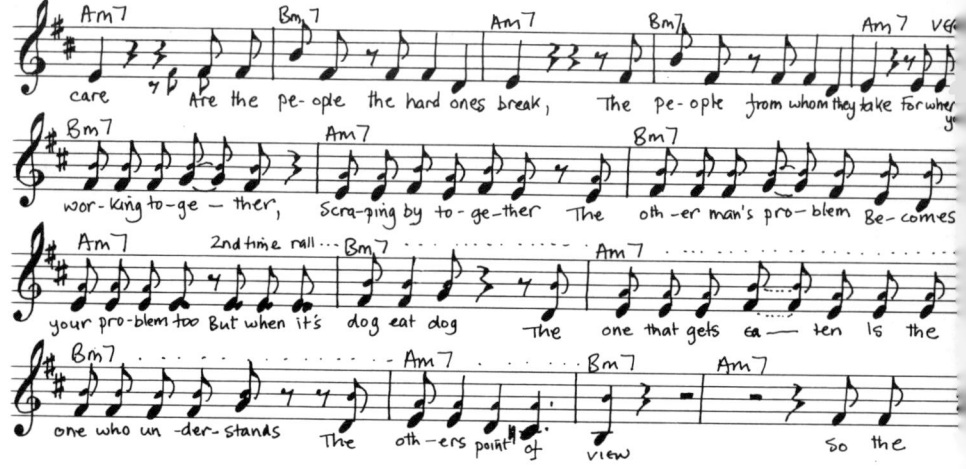

REUNION

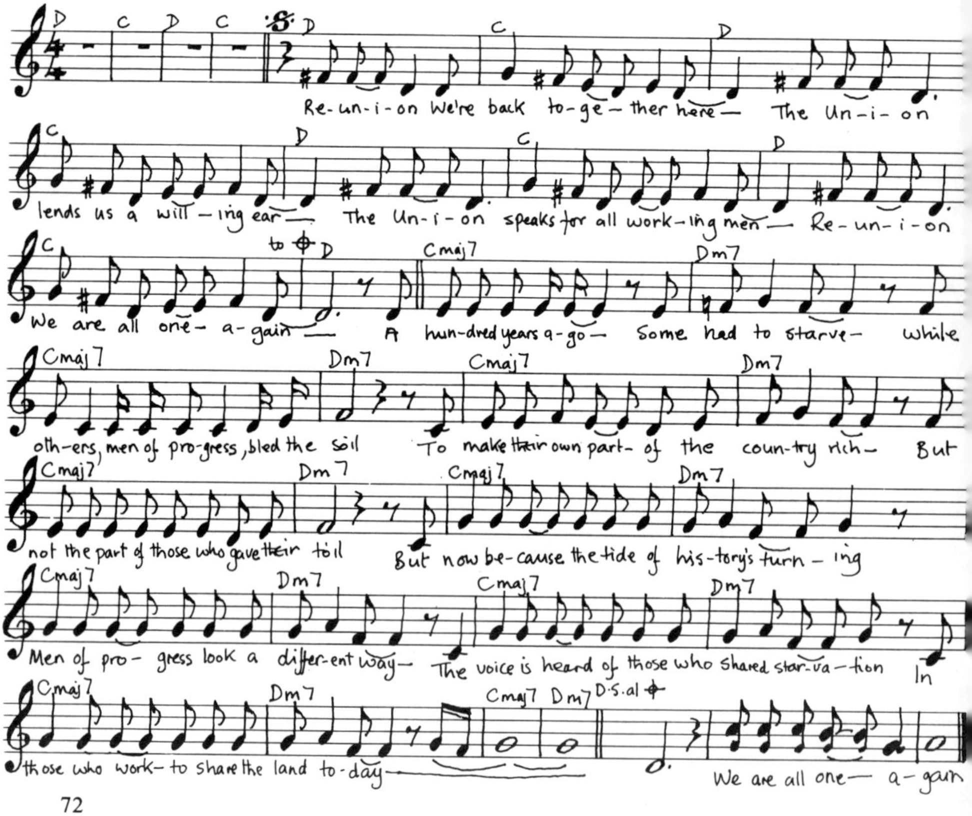

72

GET AWAY FROM THE DISHES

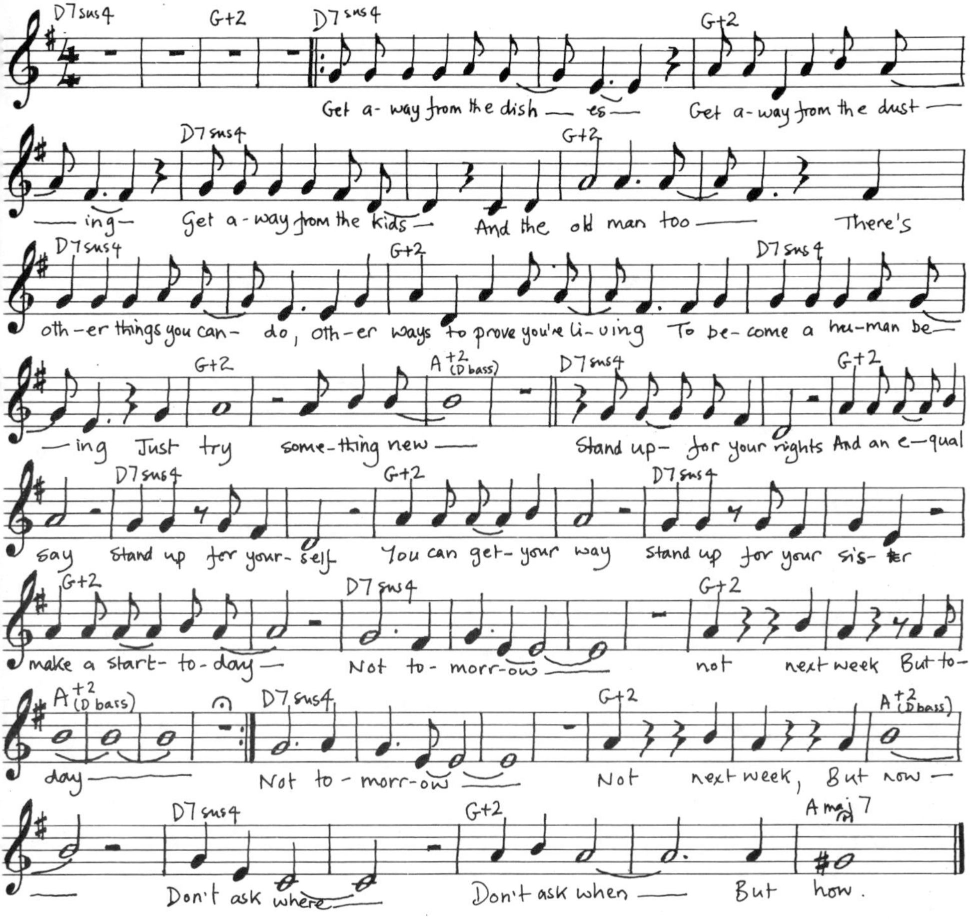

WE'RE MAKING IT KNOWN

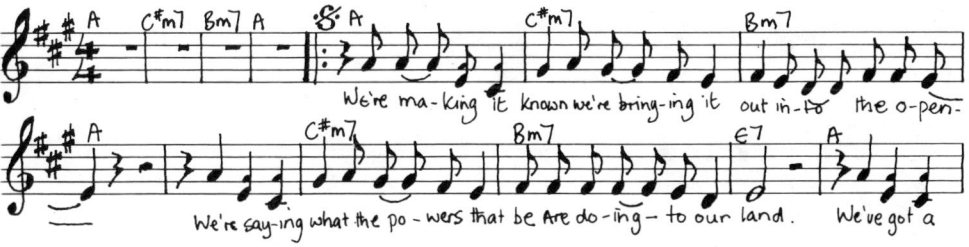

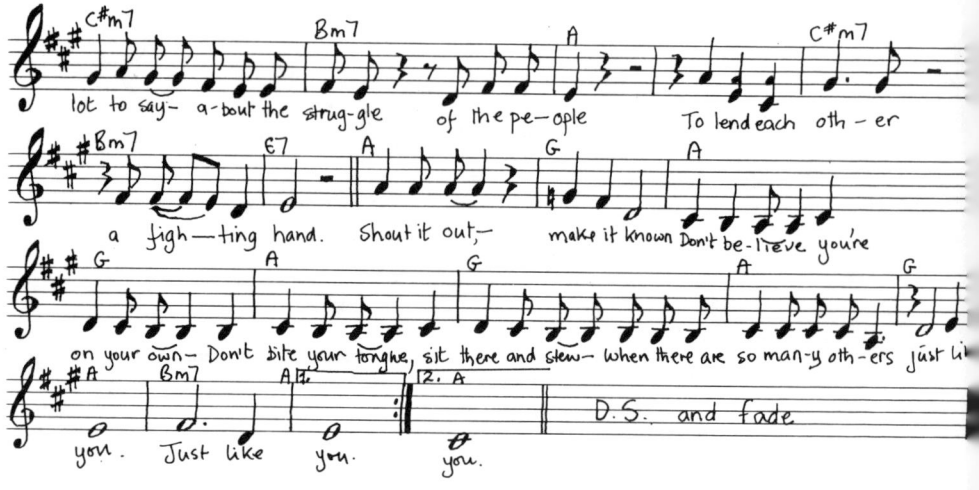

IT'S THERE, WE'RE HERE

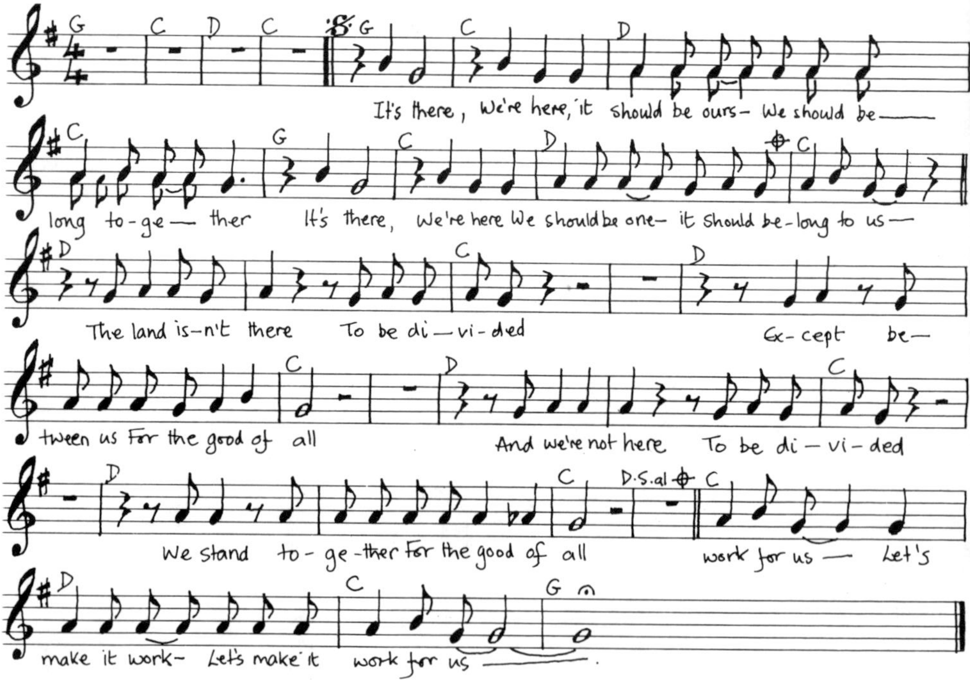